PAPERMAKING
FOR
PRINTMAKERS

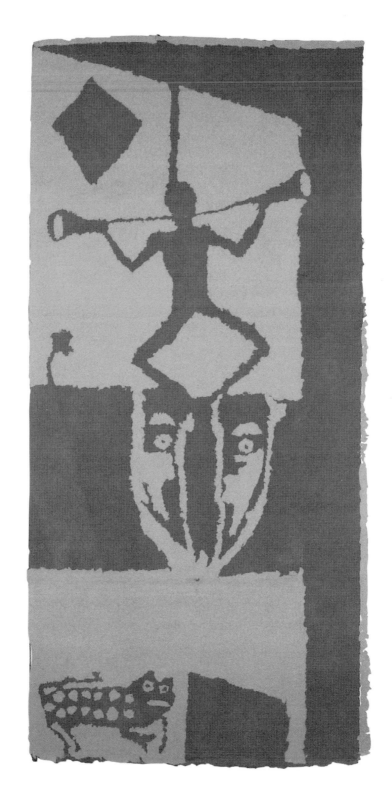

PAPERMAKING FOR PRINTMAKERS

Elspeth Lamb

A & C BLACK · LONDON

First published in Great Britain in 2006
A & C Black Publishers Limited
38 Soho Square
London W1D 3HB
www.acblack.com

ISBN-10: 0-7136-6587-4

ISBN-13: 978-0-7136-6587-1

CIP Catalogue records for this book are
available from the British Library and the
U.S. Library of Congress.

Elspeth Lamb has asserted her right
under the Copyright, Design and Patents
Act, 1988, to be identified as the author
of this work.

Book design by Susan McIntyre
Cover design by
    Sutchinda Rangsi Thompson
Copyedited and proofread by
    Julian Beecroft
Project Manager: Susan Kelly
Editorial Assistant: Sophie Page

Printed and bound in China by C&C
Offset Printing Co., Ltd.

FRONTISPIECE Elspeth Lamb; *Anasazi*; handmade dyed-cotton paper; 160 x 76 cm
(63 x 30 in.). Made at the Paper
Workshop, Glasgow, in collaboration with
master papermaker Jacki Parry.

CONTENTS

ACKNOWLEDGEMENTS

It goes without saying that a book of this nature is largely dependent on the help and generosity of those people who have the knowledge needed to make it a reality. Thus I am indebted to the following people for their input: Eileen Foti and Charmian Pollok, for their unerring support and for contributing chapters packed with information; Professor Lynne Allen, Director of RCIPP, for generously granting me the use of facilities at the excellent Centre for Innovative Print and Paper at Rutgers University; Anne McKeown at RCIPP, who also contributed a chapter on three-dimensional papermaking and offered help and guidance along with her students; and Professor Judy Brodsky, founder of RCIPP, for permission to reproduce images from their slide archive of collaborative works.

Thanks are also due to Marabeth Cohen-Tyler for the wonderful images she provided from past collaborative projects at Ken Tyler's extraordinary workshop – some of these images were the original inspiration for this book.

Megan Moorhouse of Dieu Donné Papermill in New York City has offered much encouragement and valuable advice, and Mina Takahashi, also of Dieu Donné, graciously let me loose in their slide archive.

Thanks also to Donna Koretsky and Shannon Brock at Carriage House Paper; Marje Devon, Director of the Tamarind Institute of Lithography at the University of New Mexico; Susan Macin-Dolin, for introducing me to the artists and print methods of Mixografia Workshop in Los Angeles, and for introducing me to artists across the USA; and Doug Roberts at Mixografia, for his cooperation.

Okuda-san, master papermaker from Awaji Island in Japan, deserves a mention for introducing me to the wonders of *washi*; as do Keiko Kadota and Masahiro Kosaka from the Nagasawa Art Park Programme, Japan, where I first became interested in Japanese papermaking; John Risseuw, Peggy Prentice and Georgia Deal generously gave information on how to make handmade paper for printing on; and Stephen Hutt of Smith Anderson and Co., Fettykil Mills, Scotland, donated materials for experimentation.

The images in this book have been, for the main part, generously provided by the aforementioned sources, but I would also like to extend my thanks to those individual artists who took the trouble and time to send me images of their work.

INTRODUCTION

L iving as we do in a digital age, a book that addresses a physical process such as papermaking will almost certainly be regarded by some as retrograde. I would prefer to view the following as a tactile revolt against the limitations of the flat, one-dimensional print, which seems to be appearing in ever-increasing numbers in fine-art degree shows I've seen in recent years. There is always the argument that the computer is 'just another tool' or a 'digital darkroom'. However, there is also the unadmitted fact that it is far less hassle to play around in Photoshop to produce a delightfully quick image; the alternative is to spend forever lugging impossibly heavy pieces of limestone around a rented studio, not to mention spending hours graining them, before you can even begin to draw. I have done both.

This book deals in the main part with papermaking, and as such is intended to be an introduction to that art form and how it may be used specifically in combination with print. My intention has been to aim the book specifically at the printmaker with little, or indeed no, prior knowledge of papermaking. Finding myself in a near-similar situation when I was first approached to write this handbook will, I hope, mean that my approach is sympathetic to the novice. Whilst not professing to be a professional papermaker, I am an artist and printmaker of some 25 years' experience with an abiding curiosity about paper as substrate.

Paper is seductive. I will never forget the experience of the warm basmati scent which wafted its way through the converted fire station – our improvised studio in Japan – where my colleague Kazumi and I peeled newly dried sheets of soft blue kozo from boards lovingly polished and treated with persimmon oil.

Many fine, in-depth and concise books have already been written on the subject of paper and its properties (see the bibliography at the end of this book for some of the best). Particular mention should go to the extraordinarily thorough and exhaustive research of the American Dard Hunter during the first half of the 20th century. I found his books never less than fascinating, and a valuable source of information, indeed a godsend, during the time I spent researching the history and techniques of papermaking.

I hope my own book will give artists and printmakers a taste of what can be achieved with research, experimentation and hard work. However, the subject of paper is vast, and this book can in no way contain every

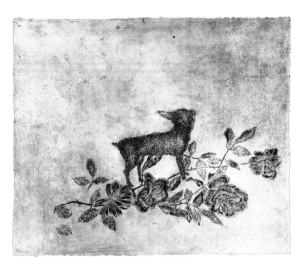

Kiki Smith, *Regalo*, 2003; mixografia print on handmade paper. Courtesy of the artist and Mixografía®.

recipe, or each type of plant or raw material involved in the making of a sheet. It will, I hope, provide an insight into new ways of creation by showing the myriad possibilities achievable when two techniques, that is, print and handmade paper, merge to create one artwork.

During the last 30 years or so, artists have changed their ways of working with paper, inasmuch as they are now working 'in' rather than 'on' the surface, thereby creating works in which the paper often becomes the object itself. This particular way of image-making – merging print with specially prepared paper substrate – seems to me to be a process most particular to the USA. Thus, most of the material for this book has been gleaned from American sources.

Printmaking by its very nature is a medium most suited to the process of building up an image in layers. It is the fusion of print with a specifically prepared and dyed sheet of paper, which can result in a work of extraordinary richness and beauty. This was confirmed to me when I first encountered print and handmade paper fused together, with spectacular results, at an exhibition entitled Printmakers' Impressions shown in the Albuquerque Museum, New Mexico during 1990. Held to celebrate the 30th anniversary of the Tamarind Lithography Workshop, the exhibition was directly linked to a symposium held at the Tamarind Institute of Lithography, Albuquerque, University of New Mexico, which attracted printmakers from all over the world.

The prints in question – a Frank Stella image combining relief, screen-printing, etching, woodcut and hand-colouring on a specially prepared pulp sheet, and an eight-by-ten foot James Rosenquist pressed paper-pulp image combined with lithography and collage – were magnificent in both scale and execution. They seemed to vibrate with a brilliancy of richness and colour hitherto unseen in the world of printmaking. Both had been produced at Tyler Graphics Ltd, Ken Tyler's extraordinary workshop at Mount Kisko, New York State.

The undoubted high spot at the start of my research was being invited out to lunch one icy February in 2003 with June Wayne, the founder of the aforementioned, seminal, and now world-famous, Tamarind Institute of Lithography. I had been generously granted the opportunity of doing some research within the Rutgers Center for Innovative Print and Paper at Mason Gross School of the Arts, Rutgers University. We went to the Elks Club, a men's club that had previously excluded women from its premises. My three companions – June, Eileen Foti (master printer) and Anne McKeown (papermaker), both tutors at the Rutgers Center – were stimulating and formidable company.

What impressed me most about these indomitable women was their abiding passion for original print and paper. Many issues were discussed that cold February lunchtime: last, but not least, the post-9/11 world crisis and the ever-ominous threat of war with Iraq. The conversation returned to print and paper, which we discussed at some length. We resolved to try, as artists and educators, to keep these processes, and our shared passion for them, alive.

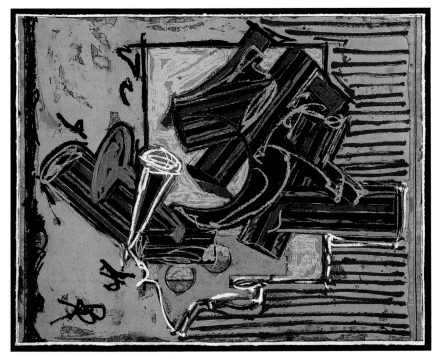

Frank Stella; *La penna di hu*; 55½ x 66 in.; relief, etching, woodcut, screenprint, stencil, hand-coloured. © Frank Stella/Tyler Graphics Ltd/Artists Rights Society (ARS), New York; 1988.

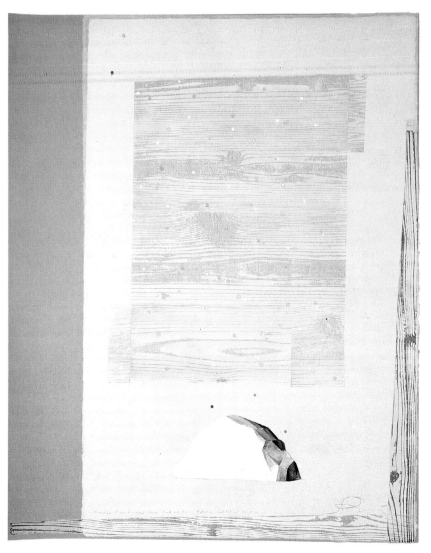

Shoichi Ida, *Winter – Mitate,* from the *Surface is the Between – Between Vertical and Horizontal* series. Woodblock print with watercolour, on two layers of paper (*Echizen kozo usu kizuki* and *Echizen kozo atu kizuki*); 97 x 77 cm (38 x 30⅓ in.); © Shoichi Ida; 1986.

1 · PAPER AND PRINT: EARLY BEGINNINGS

Writing materials

It is generally surmised that stone was probably the first material to be engraved with figures and letters, as demonstrated by Egyptian hieroglyphics. Alternative writing materials included bones, wood, clay, bricks, metals such as lead, and wax tablets. In pre-Homeric times, marks were scratched into wood coated with wax, chalk or plaster to create text. According to Pliny the Elder, men first wrote on the leaves of palm trees: hence our contemporary use of the word 'leaf' to denote a page in a book. The early Romans used the inner bark, or *liber*, of the tree as a writing material, thereby introducing the word 'library' into contemporary language.

In the early Christian era, monks would painstakingly illuminate manuscripts on parchment or vellum, a material made from the skin of young animals. Apparently, skins from around 500 sheep were required to produce the parchment for the Domesday Book, written in AD 1086.

In China and Japan printing from woodblocks was preceded by the use of seals. The use of incised seals to make an impression with pigment upon paper was, to some degree, a form of printing. There are also examples of stamped or printed cloth and leather preserved in Japanese temples dating from the first half of the 8th century. Around AD 770, a Japanese empress named Shotoku reputedly sanctioned the printing of one million paper prayers, known as the Million Charms. The project, which took several years to complete, probably signifies the second oldest example of text printed on paper.

The development of calligraphy by ancient Chinese scholars hastened the need for a writing material that was more economical, and easier to write upon, than cloth. It should be noted that Oriental paper, being made for writing upon, had a soft surface to receive ink from a calligraphic brush. Interestingly, the Japanese, Chinese and Koreans used wood as a paper fibre before Western papermakers. In Europe, paper had to be different in composition from papers produced in the East, to accommodate inks such as ox-gall and lampblack. European paper also used rags as opposed to vegetable fibres.

Relief

The earliest printed images were relief prints, or woodcuts. The process takes its name from the fact that the printing surface is raised above its background. In India, Buddhism enabled this method of printing to evolve through what became known as 'block-book printing'.

Coloured papers

During the 14th century, what became known as 'prepared paper' was introduced for making a coloured background for a drawing. Colour was added to the white paper by applying a watercolour wash. This method, however, created problems when it came to printing, as the brushed-on colour sometimes flaked off when printing ink was introduced to the surface. The alternative to this method of colouring paper was simply to dye the basic material, in this case rags, to introduce colour. From the 13th up until the 18th century, indigo dye was introduced to make coloured paper. By the 18th century, dye was being added directly to the pulp while it was being beaten. This is the method most commonly used today.

THE ORIGINS OF PAPER

Pulp fiction: who invented it?

In the history of world civilisation, the development of paper plays an important role. This simple material has become a necessary part of our existence, and to be without it would be simply unthinkable. Taken for granted, it has, ironically, become invisible. However, we could not survive contemporary life without money, phone directories, stamps, travel tickets and the like.

The name 'paper' originates from the Latin *papyrus*, the first material to closely resemble paper as a substrate. Paper and papyrus are made in different ways, but generally look the same. The main difference is that paper is made from macerated fibres; true paper must be made from disintegrated fibre. Traditional papyrus, on the other hand, was made by overlapping cut sections of the stalk into lengths and then laminating them together. The Egyptians used the resultant material as a substrate for hieroglyphic writings from as early as 3500 BC.

Over subsequent millennia, various raw materials have been investigated, including esparto, cotton, hemp, manila, jute and flax. The first-known experiments to produce paper as we know it today are accredited to a Chinese court official, Ts'ai Lun, from Lei-yang, in Hunan province, who announced his invention to the Emperor in AD105. He had reduced a mixture of boiled rags, fishing nets and the bark of the mulberry tree to fibre. Tests conducted by the British Museum indicate that early Chinese paper was of a very high quality. Some historians have argued that paper was invented at least two centuries earlier, and archaeologists have discovered substances resembling paper in such areas as Baqiao dating between 49 and 8 BC. However, it is generally accepted that Ts'ai Lun probably refined the papermaking process, produced paper sheets and promoted paper as a writing material. Not only that: initial papermaking experiments using disintegrated cloth, mulberry, hemp and grass plants were taken up at a later stage.

The sting

It should also be noted that any substance that pre-dates Ts'ai Lun's discoveries that bears any resemblance to paper must be attributed to wasps from the Vespidae family, usually referred to as paper wasps. This tiny insect produces paper pulp by macerating fibres in its mouth and regurgitating pulpy fibres from inside its body, in order to connect the fibres of its nest. The plant fibres that supply the wasp with raw material can consist of wooden fencing, grasses and old paper. In 1720, the French scientist Réamur, having observed the insect in this process, speculated that if a wasp could produce a paper-like substance out of plant fibre then surely humans could too.

The Orient and beyond

Papermaking was introduced into Japan in about AD 610, when the process was passed along the trade routes. At this time, Japan was undergoing a profound cultural change. The country was under the influence of China, considered then to be intellectually the most highly developed country in the world. From China and Japan, knowledge of the process passed along the old Silk Route through Samarkand, Arabia and Egypt to Morocco.

The technique entered Europe by way of Spain around 1150. European papermakers made use of old rags for making pulp, which had the advantage of being quicker to beat than, for example, hemp.

The earliest reference to England's first mill, whose products were used for an edition of Chaucer's *Canterbury Tales*, appears in a book printed by Caxton around 1490. In Scotland, small mills were also established near

Edinburgh during the reign of James VI (James I of England) at the beginning of the 17th century.

Until printing from movable type was invented around 1450, there was not much demand for paper. However, by the 18th century there were thousands of mills in operation. These two inventions, papermaking and printing, developed along parallel lines, and the mills, using traditional methods of production, found it increasingly difficult to supply enough paper to service demand.

In Britain, the early mills were not always a success, as it was reckoned that the discarded rags used by papermakers carried disease in the form of the plague. At this stage, the highest-quality sheets were creamy- or greyish-coloured, since there was an absence of chemicals in their manufacture, while lower-quality paper was often brown or grey, and speckled in appearance. Linen and cotton rags were used as the raw materials for papermaking until 1800; it was only after this date that the practice of bleaching cotton rag and linen to be used in papermaking was adopted.

In the second half of the 18th century, the effects of the Industrial Revolution were felt indirectly within the paper industry. The Georgian era was a literary one, and the educated population bought many more books, so paper was in demand; newspapers had also started to evolve, and demand outstripped supply. The Napoleonic Wars later added another difficulty by making it difficult to import raw materials.

Although there was no national free education in England until 1870, there was still a greater demand for schoolbooks and writing materials. Voluntary schooling through religious and charitable bodies also increased demand for paper with the result that, by the end of the 18th century, high-quality paper sheets were being produced by hand.

HOW THE FIRST SHEETS WERE MADE

Beating paper

A pestle and mortar is the earliest-known method for beating vegetable matter or wood fibre. Mixing the base fibre with water ensured easy maceration. After beating, the material was placed in water and stirred. The stirring action then separated out the fibres.

The Hollander beater

In 1718 Leonhard Christoff Sturm produced a book on engineering which contained illustrations of the first Hollander beater. However, it is reckoned that the beater was already in use in Holland in the 1670s, hence its name. This prototype operated in much the same way as those being used today.

The invention of the papermaking machine

In 1798 a Frenchman, Nicolas Louis Robert, produced one of the first papermaking machines. The machine was unfortunately not a success, but the concept was passed to the Fourdrinier brothers, who ran a stationery firm in London. Their machine, based on the Robert model but with many modifications, succeeded where the earlier one had failed. It became known as the Fourdrinier, or cylinder, machine, and is responsible for most paper produced in a continuous roll.

Early moulds

The earliest sheets produced in China, as well as all the papers produced in Europe until the invention of the paper machine, were formed individually by hand. It is likely that this was achieved initially by pouring the pulp solution into a 'wove'-style mould. This mould was probably a four-sided bamboo frame over which was stretched a piece of woven cloth. To prevent the pulp from slipping off the sides of the mould when it was pulled up through the water, early papermakers held sticks along its edges. This was the prototype of the deckle, a box-like structure introduced to fit neatly on top of the mould. The word originates from the German *Deckel*, meaning 'cover'.

Different materials, such as bamboo, oak, mahogany, fig and pine, were also used to make these moulds. The moulds with the newly formed sheets were laid out to dry in the sun. Wove moulds consisting of a woven mesh surface developed later in the 18th century, and sheets formed on these tended to be smoother in appearance. The inventor of wove paper was an Englishman, John Baskerville, who published his first book, *Virgil*, in 1757. This was printed onto wove paper made by the James Whatman paper mill.

The mould and deckle

The next significant development in the papermaking process was the invention of the 'laid' mould. This involved the pulp being submerged in a vat of water, and the sieve-like mould and deckle being dipped into the vat of pulp, or 'stuff', so as to scoop up, or 'pull', a sheet of wet paper. Today, the process of sheet forming is the same. Holding the mould just above the surface of the water having scooped up a quantity of pulp from the vat, the papermaker quickly shakes the mould skilfully from side to side then back and forward to allow the pulp to settle evenly across the mould. This action allows the fibres to interweave.

The wet sheet of paper can then be removed from the mould by pressing it face down onto a dampened felt, thus enabling the papermaker to produce further sheets, as many as are needed, from the same mould. This action is known as 'couching' the sheet (from the French verb *coucher*, to lay (something) down). Early European paper was also air-dried, though in this case over horsehair ropes as opposed to, say, the Japanese tradition of drying sheets on boards. Early 14th-century paper reveals coarse laid lines when held to the light. The wire used at this time was 'cut' wire. Drawn wire was a later, more refined product. The wires were laid on the surface of the mould and then chain was stitched to the ribs of the mould, spaced at intervals of roughly an inch – hence the term 'chain lines' to describe them.

European moulds

Today, the European mould is a fixed wooden mould quite unlike that used in the Far East, the *su*, which has a flexible hinged frame with a removable mesh. Western moulds are rectangular-shaped frames, rather like picture frames in appearance, and of two sorts, already described: the laid and the wove.

Raw materials in Europe

Rags – for example, linen and cotton – were washed, then allowed to ferment in water for around six weeks in order to loosen the fibres. These were then cut and beaten – initially between two rocks, later with the use of a pestle and mortar – to macerate the fibres. The resulting pulp was placed in a vat with a good volume of water and stirred freely, allowing the fibres to separate. Stamping machines were also used, which consisted of a row of water-powered hammers, some with sharp iron teeth to fray the rags.

Eastern papermaking.

There are two methods of making paper in Japan; *tame-zuki* and *nagashi-zuki*. *Tame-zuki* is the method that most closely resembles Western papermaking.

Historically, the Japanese sheet-forming method *tame-zuki* is recorded during the Heian Period from 794–1192 as using plants such as *gampi*, *kozo*, *kurara* and flax to make paper. Raw material was prepared by cutting it into small pieces, boiling it in wood ash, removing specks and beating it in a mortar. After beating, the pulp was then put into the papermaking vat, from which it could be scooped up onto the screen. After forming, the wet sheet was then transferred to a piece of cloth.

Nagashi-zuki method – the contemporary Japanese process of making paper

(Please refer to *Oriental sheet-forming* on p.44 for an indepth description.)

In the modern *nagashi-zuki* method of papermaking, a mucous substance called *neri* is added to the pulp. *Neri* is extracted from the *tororo-aoi* root. *Tororo-aoi* (*Hibiscus manihot*) is an annual herbaceous plant of the mallow (*Malvaceae*) family.

The roots are crushed to produce the *neri* mucilage. Adding the *neri*, also known as 'formation aid', to the pulp in the vat ensures a slow drainage during sheet-forming, allowing time for the fibres to align themselves evenly, resulting in a smooth sheet of even thickness. *Neri* also enhances the lustre in many bast fibres.

During sheet formation, the stock pulp is scooped up several times into the paper mould. After the first scoop, sometimes referred to as 'throwing the wave', another charge of the stock pulp is scooped up immediately, and the papermaker keeps the mould moving back and forth, sometimes moving it from side to side. This procedure continues without any pausing between scoops until a good layer of fibre has accumulated on the surface of the mould.

Japanese papermaking moulds are known as *sugeta* or *suketa*, and consist of two parts. The specially-made, flexible, removable screen, or *su*, consists of very thin splints of either bamboo or miscanthus (*Miscanthus sinensis*), which is a tall perennial pampas grass. *Su* made of pampas were much more common prior to 1300, when horsehair was used instead of silk.

The bamboo used in the making of the screen is either black bamboo (*Phyllostachys puberilla*) or long-jointed bamboo (*Phyllostachys bambusoides*) stitched together by silk or, more recently, nylon threads. These threads are treated with persimmon tannin for wet strength. The number

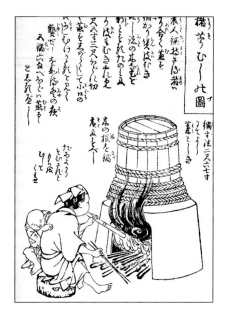

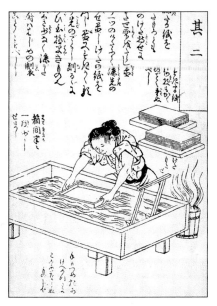

Steaming *kozo* faggots to loosen bark; from the Kamisuki Chohoki.

Forming sheets of paper in the vat; from the Kamisuki Chohoki. Both images courtesy Glasgow University Library, Department of Special Collections.

of bamboo strips varies according to what kind of paper is to be made. The diameter of the ribs can be anything in the range 0.5-0.7 mm. The hinged wooden frame, or *keta,* holds the *su* in place. The *keta* is usually made from Japanese cypress wood. These screens leave impressions on the formed sheets that are often referred to as laid lines.

Oriental papers

> *'Western paper turns away the light, while our paper seems to take it in, to envelop it gently, like the soft surface of a first snowfall. It gives off no sound when it is crumpled or folded, it is quiet and pliant to the touch, as the leaf of a tree.'*

Japanese fibre possesses several unique qualities. Apart from its inherent beauty, the paper, when formed, appears very delicate, but is in fact deceptively strong. This is because the fibre retains a 3-12 mm length, even after beating. By comparison, rag or wood pulps are 4 mm or less.

The first paper to appear in Japan, in the 8th century, was made from mulberry bark (*Broussonetia papyrifera*) followed by a wild-growing shrub, *gampi*, of which several varieties, including *Wikstroemia canescens* and

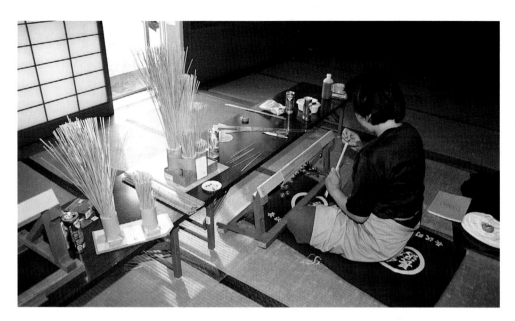

Weaving a Japanese *su* using *miscanthus*

Diplomorpha sikokiana, are used in papermaking.

Gampi is a low-growth deciduous tree of the daphne (*Thymelaceae*) family. It is difficult to cultivate, and is often harvested in the wild. The fibre is thin, very lustrous and short, and resilient to insects, which renders it very strong. It produces excellent paper of wonderful translucency. Used for chine-collé additions for prints, it accepts ink readily and holds detail well. Due to its off-white colour, it is sometimes called *tori no ko*, which translates as 'bird's child', as the colour resembles the colour of an eggshell. It was used for copying sutras, or scriptures, during the Nara period, when it was called *hishi*.

Mitsumata (*Edgeworthia papyrifera* or *Daphne papyrifera*) has uncertain origins, but was documented as first being used to make paper around 1597. It is another low-growth deciduous tree of the Thymelaceae family. The fibre is thin and lustrous and is excellent to print on; it is also much shorter and weaker than *kozo*, but produces a denser, crisper, shinier paper. It has been used in the past to print Japanese banknotes. Other uses have included *hakuaishi* (gold-leaf interleaf paper.)

Asa (*Cannabis sativa (L.)*), a member of the mulberry (*Moraceae*) family known as hemp, was plentiful but required laborious preparation, so its usage dwindled.

Kozo (*Broussonetia kazinoki*) is a low-growth deciduous tree of the mulberry family. Several varieties are used for papermaking. Having thick, long and strong fibres, it is often used for *shojigami* (Japanese screens) and art and calligraphy paper. Nowadays, *kozo* is by far the most common fibre to be used in Japanese papers. It is also excellent for printing *mokuhan* (Japanese woodblock prints), as it can hold several layers of water-based inks or paints.

Bamboo and rice straw were used in Japanese papermaking for centuries, but are rarely used today. (It should be noted here that ricepaper has nothing to do with Japanese handmade paper.)

Harvesting and preparation of the fibres

For information on modern and traditional methods of Japanese papermaking, refer to the excellent and comprehensive manual, *Japanese Papermaking*, by Timothy Barrett (see Bibliography).

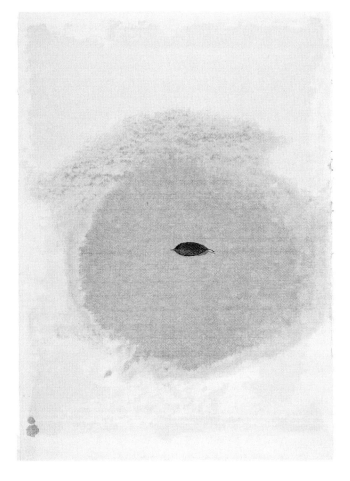

Shoichi Ida, *Surface Is the Between – Between Vertical and Horizon* series: *Paper Between Leaf and Pond*, 100 x 70 cm (39⅓ x 27½ in.); kozo handmade paper and Fabriano; screenprint/lithograph with *chine collé*; printed on both sides of the paper.

2 · SETTING UP

THE GATHERING OF MATERIALS

For the hand-papermaker, the raw materials for papermaking can be loosely divided into three categories of fibre types: raw plant fibres, prepared fibres and recycled materials.

Fibre categories:

1. Raw plant fibres

Raw plant fibres for papermaking can either be purchased dried from specialist papermaking suppliers or gathered fresh by the papermaker from his or her own environment, whether town or country. Suppliers of fibres for textile artists are also a good source of dried raw fibres, e.g., flax.

If you have a garden or a window box, then plants can be grown for papermaking. Even in cities the papermaker has access to fibres by purchasing suitable flowers or by buying vegetables such as leek or celery. Enquire if your local grocer has any old produce which could be utilised, or ask your nearest parks department if they ever have any waste plant matter.

Plants can be harvested at more than one time of the year. However, in general, if you are harvesting plants in the countryside, take them in the autumn after the growing season, leaving the roots in the ground if the plant is a herbaceous perennial. If you are using garden shrubs take prunings, and, if using something like silver birch, take young branches about one and a half to two inches maximum diameter. In some woody plants like broom or heather the stems will be much smaller in diameter. These will need further treatment before processing, such as steaming and stripping, which will be covered later on in this section. Plants such as nettle can be harvested after the stalks have overwintered, when much of the fleshy, non-cellulose material which you do not need has naturally rotted away from the plant – a process known as 'retting', which cuts down on the need to add chemicals (see section on preparation of fibres) You can then collect the stems and tie them in bundles to be hung in a dry place until they are needed. Other plants, such as soft rush or the common reed, can also be dried and stored, although in the wet west of Scotland soft rush seems to grow happily almost all year, especially in the recent milder winters. Sometimes, fibres such as those of kozo or silver birch need to be steamed and stripped. Plants such as hollyhock or nasturtium can be left through the winter to dry in the ground in your garden. Harvest these when the natural retting process has taken place, making sure the plant material is dry before storing it.

Be environmentally aware, and also note that it is illegal in some countries to pick wild plants. By picking stems or leaves of perennial plants that have died back in the autumn or winter, e.g., the common reed, you are not destroying the plant. If you are harvesting fibres on private land, you must obviously seek the permission of the landowner. Allow a plant to do its growing and seed-setting before harvesting, and remove as little as possible. When using trees and shrubs from a garden, collect your papermaking fibres at the same time as the plant is pruned. Experimentation will teach you which plants are best for papermaking. Raw plant fibres can, themselves, be divided into categories depending on which part of the plant they come from. Fibres marked with an asterisk* are available in various part-processed forms from papermaking suppliers. The categories are as follows:

Bast fibres (inner-bark fibres): this category can be further subdivided into three sections:

Woody bast fibres	e.g. *kozo**, *gampi**, silver birch
Herbaceous bast fibres	e.g. nettle, flax*
Petiole bast fibres	e.g. abaca*

The term 'bast' covers fibres found in that part of the plant lying between the outer bark and the inner, woody core, and also refers to fibres from the stalks of both annual and perennial herbaceous plants and to petiole-bast fibres. The petiole is the leaf stalk of a plant.

Leaf fibres: iris, daffodil, yucca, pineapple, leek, etc.

Grass fibres: esparto*, rush, pampas grass, bamboo*
Note that although esparto is listed as a grass fibre you would use the stalks and leaves. With pampas grass, the part you would use is the leaf and sometimes the seeds. See the chapter on plant pulps.

Seed fibres: cotton* is the main seed fibre used.
Thistledown seeds can be used on their own but may be best employed mixed in with a base pulp to give added strength. Adding them to recycled *gampi* pulp gives a wonderfully lustrous and fine pulp, but adding some to either cotton or abaca is also effective. Experiment!

2. Part-processed fibres

Cotton linters are usually available in the form of compressed and dried sheets of pulp, often called 'linters'. The word 'linters' is actually the name of the machine used in processing the cotton fibres from the plant, although it is often used to describe sheets of other pre-prepared plant pulps. You may also see these sheets referred to as 'half-stuff' or even just 'pulp'.

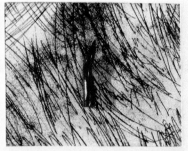

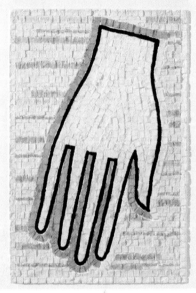

Linters resemble thick sheets of white blotting paper, and are pre-washed and boiled. They can be used to replace 5-35% of the rag content of fine papers with little or no loss of strength, and may be dyed prior to beating, dyed in the Hollander whilst beating, or mixed with other pulp materials. Linters mix well with other pulp such as abaca to form sheets for printing, and they can also be used to cast paper.

A good catalogue, such as that produced by Carriage House in New York, will always explain what form each type of 'fibre' takes and how much processing needs to be

Mimmo Paladino; *California Suite No. 1*, 2004. Mixografia print on handmade paper. Courtesy of the artist and Mixografía®.

done to it. These firms will also be happy to answer queries, as will sellers of fine papers such as Falkiner Fine Papers. The following types of fibre are available:

Abaca (Manila, or Manila Hemp) is a bast fibre which comes from the leaf stalk of a banana plant (*Musa textilis*) that is native to the Philippines. Abaca produces translucent sheets similar to Japanese paper if beaten for a long time in a Hollander beater. It has high shrinkage, so is also suitable for making paper sculpture. It can be purchased from paper suppliers in the form of pre-processed sheet pulp.

Bamboo (*Phyllostachys aurea*) comes from the stem of the bamboo plant.

Blue-jeans pulp is available as reclaimed fibres to be cooked and beaten, or in sheet form from Carriage House, New York, and makes very strong paper.

Esparto grass the Spanish variety of this plant has strong fibres and produces white pulp. Grass fibres such as bamboo and rice straw can also be used.

Eucalyptus may be environmentally doubtful.

Hemp originates in Asia. It contains a fibre of high cellulose content, with good length and strength. It makes a white, lustrous paper that was first produced in China during the 1st century AD.

Kraft paper is a type of recycled paper available from paper mills, and can be purchased from Falkiner Fine Papers in London.

Ramie is also known as China grass, rhea or grasscloth plant, and is classed as a cellulose fibre. One of the oldest of all vegetable fibres, it was used for Chinese burial shrouds over 2, 000 years ago. Ramie fibre is fine and silk-like, with a high lustre, and the fibre is located in the bark of the stalk.

Rice straw produces a fast-draining, short-fibred pulp.

Sabai is a grass pulp from Nepal.

Sisal (*Agave sisalana*) is a desert succulent from Central and South America that gives high-quality papermaking pulp.

Thai kozo is available cooked, cleaned & bleached from Carriage House, New York, but in limited supply.

All the pulps, sold as flat, dried, part-processed sheets of fibres, are ready to be soaked and beaten. The use of these part-prepared fibres takes a lot of the hard work out of the process, making them ideal for someone working either at home or without access to a specialist papermaking studio. To use, tear the sheets into smallish pieces and soak them overnight. If you find some of the sheets tough and difficult to tear up, rip them into large pieces and soak these overnight. You should then find it easy to tear them down into pieces small enough for whichever beating method you are going to use. See the following section on Beating.

3. Recycled materials

When making paper by hand there are several things to be considered. Firstly, the papers may be heavily printed on; or they may be glossy and coated like magazine paper; or they may be heavily sized. Also, newspaper, or any paper containing a high proportion of wood pulp, will be very acidic and thus prone to rapid deterioration. Using just a proportion of this type of recycled paper along with a base of, say, cotton linters or abaca pulp will yield a stronger and more useful pulp. Be aware that a lot of this paper will already have been recycled; you cannot go on recycling indefinitely, as the cellulose fibres become shorter and shorter each time.

As printmakers, however, you will probably have access to offcuts from high-quality printing papers, and these can be recycled, perhaps with small quantities added of handmade vegetable or plant pulps. This way you will achieve unique and distinctive papers. Check when using these offcuts whether the paper was sized; this will affect whether you choose to size the resulting pulp. If you are using one of the well-known printing papers, this information should be easily available from papermaking catalogues or paper suppliers.

In Europe, traditionally, rags were recycled to make paper, principally from linen (which comes from flax), but also from cotton. If you have access to a Hollander beater, you can easily produce wonderfully crisp paper of high quality from old linen clothing or bedding. A recipe is given under the Cooking section of this chapter.

PRECOOKING PREPARATION

Paper is made from fibres formed from cellulose, which is found in the cell walls of plants and gives them structure. There are many other substances found in plants that need to be got rid of – for example, pectins, starches, waxes, lignin – because they can cause deterioration. These are broken down by cooking the plant in an alkaline substance.

Pre-soaking

All plants benefit from being soaked in water overnight (longer if they are tough) before being cooked. This will help to cut down the time the plants need to be cooked with alkalis. Plants that are especially tough can also be soaked in an alkaline solution prior to being cooked. In some countries, for instance, fibres are left soaking in lime to free the cellulose. In this

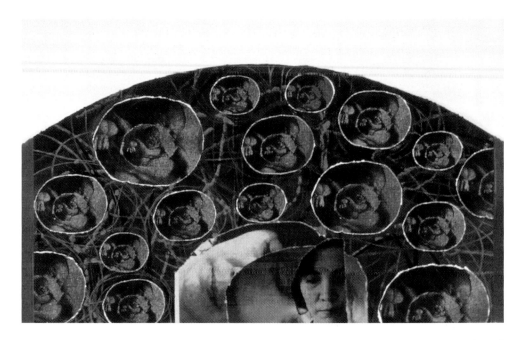

Juan Sanchez, *Cries and Pain,* 2000. Photo and hand-drawn silkscreen and water-based monoprint on shaped handmade cotton paper with paper-pulp painting, mounted on · mat board. 68.5 x 134.5 cm (27 x 53 in.). Courtesy of the artist, Dieu Donné Papermill, and Lower East Side Printshop.

case drain off the old alkali before making a new solution for the cooking process.

Prior to the cooking process, some plants need extra preparation in the form of steaming, stripping or scraping of the outer skin – for example, pineapple leaves, broom, heather – or by the previously mentioned retting. Woody plants that will yield bast fibres will probably need to be steamed before the inner bark can be separated from the inner core. Where possible, the outer bark will need to be scraped off, though this is not necessary with petiole bast fibres.

Retting

With herbaceous bast fibres such as nettle, follow the natural retting process by allowing the plant to stand over the winter, letting the weather naturally rot away the unwanted parts of the plant. Natural retting also works really well with leaf fibres such as crocosmia.

Retting is really a process of fermentation that takes place as bacterial action works on the fleshy materials. You can encourage this process by soaking tough plants in water – black rubbish bins with a lid are ideal to hold a large quantity of soaking fibres. The lid is essential for blocking out the light, though you don't want to exclude all the air. If it smells unpleasant then the process is working. It is also possible to add extra substances such as milk or beer to accelerate the process. Helen Hiebert in *Papermaking with Plants* recommends 8 oz (240 ml) of milk per 5 q (5 l) of water. She also recommends testing the fibre regularly for 'doneness' by 'gently tugging it on its long axis. When it pulls apart, it is done.' How long this takes depends on variables such as the toughness of the plant, the ambient temperature and the vigour of the bacterial activity – so anything from a few days to several weeks. With thick, fleshy-leaved plants like pineapple or agave a period of retting is needed before you are able to scrape the leaves to get at the fibres. This scraping process is called 'decortication', for which you should use a sharp knife and a chopping board.

Retting will cut down on the need for added chemicals in the hand-papermaking process, allowing weather and bacterial activity to do the work. You can also do a controlled retting, whereby the plant is allowed to ferment in water inside a covered bin in a warm place.

FURTHER PREPARATION OF HERBACEOUS AND WOODY BAST FIBRES

Steaming

First, cut your plant parts into lengths, putting them into the largest pan you possess, assuming this also has a lid. Helen Hiebert in *Papermaking with Plants* suggests using two identically sized pans, inverting one on top of the other to serve as a lid. Fill the bottom pan with approximately 2 in. (5 cm) of water and steam until you can see the bark beginning to shrink away from the wood. This could take anything up to two hours; it could also be much quicker, so keep an eye out to make sure that the water does not boil away.

Stripping

As soon as the plant is cool enough to handle, begin stripping off the bark starting from the wider end. You may need to make a nick with a knife in the end of the bark to get it started, but pull it firmly away from the inner core and it will, hopefully, come off in one long strip. The outer bark may also flake off during this procedure.

Cleaning

If the outer bark is still on the fibre, scrape it off, keeping the inner bark moist as you do this. The purer you want your finished paper to be, the more careful you have to be to clean off the flecks of outer bark. Do this on a stout chopping board. Then rinse off the fibre in clean water to remove any remaining flecks of outer bark.

Hollow-stemmed plants

Hollow-stemmed plants such as hollyhock, nettle and soft rush need to have their stems battered with a mallet or rolling pin. Where a plant is very light, e.g. soft rush, you will have to weight it down in its soaking or cooking liquid, otherwise it will float.

Cutting into short lengths

All plants need to be cut into short lengths before cooking, either with scissors or with a garden shredder if you have one. This is especially useful if you need to process a large quantity of plant material. When handling plants you soon learn to tell what sort of preliminary treatment they will need before cooking.

COOKING WITH ALKALIS

To cook your plant material and rid it of the unwanted substances which you will rinse away at the end of cooking, leaving you with the cellulose fibres, you need to use an alkaline substance. The alkalis most commonly used in hand-papermaking are listed below. The gentler the alkaline substance used, the better for the paper, as too strong an alkali can damage it. Measure the strength of your alkaline solution by using pH-indicator strips, which are available from papermaking suppliers (see p.141). These give you a measurement on a scale ranging from 0 at the acid end to 14 at the alkali end. A pH of 7 is neutral.

Measure the amount of alkali in either of two ways: as a percentage of the dry weight of fibre or as concentration per volume of water. Approximately 8 l of water is enough for every 500 g of dry fibre. The desired pH values are given below after each chemical. Two to three hours maximum should be enough time to cook the fibres. If they have not cooked after this time, drain them off and make up a fresh alkaline solution. Next time, consider retting the plant before cooking: all fibres should be soaked overnight before cooking, as the moistened fibres take up the alkali more efficiently during cooking. Wearing gloves is advised when handling alkalis, but beware of latex allergy. Also, wear a protective apron. Make sure the cooking takes place in a well-ventilated space or even outdoors if possible.

Sodium carbonate

Also called soda ash, this is the basic chemical in washing soda. Washing soda also contains other substances, which vary from make to make and which may leave a residue on the paper. It is, however, easily available and sold as a household cleaning substance. Aim for a pH solution of between 9 and 11 for cooking.

> *Dry measurement*: 20% soda ash per 500 g (1 lb) dry fibre
> *Wet measurement*: 15 g (½ oz) per 1 l (2 pt) water

Add the measured amount of soda ash to the pot of water just before it comes to the boil, stir in – it will dissolve easily – then add the fibre.

Wood-ash lye

This is what was traditionally used in Japan. It cooks the fibres more gently than other chemicals and rinses out easily. A recipe is given on page 135. Aim for solution with a pH of between 9 and 12. Although this will already be in solution, you may need to add additional water to ensure the fibres are covered.

Lime

Used traditionally in several cultures both for retting and for cooking of fibres. Use at a pH of between 11 and 13. Can be easily dissolved in water. Since lime is less strong, the cooking time will be much longer.

Caustic soda

Sometimes known as lye, its concentration varies from country to country. This will affect its usage, so do enquire as to whether or not it is pure. Use for tough fibres that will not readily break down with soda ash. The pH will be between 12 and 14.

As its name implies, this is a very caustic substance and should be handled with care, using gloves, in a well-ventilated space. Always add the caustic soda to a small amount of cold water and then add all this to the unheated, measured cooking water before putting in the fibres. Never add the water to the caustic soda: if added to hot water it can froth up alarmingly.

Chemical	Source	Quantities
Soda ash (Na_2CO_3) (Sodium carbonate)	Papermaking, printmaking & ceramic suppliers	100 g (3¼ oz) per 500 g (1 lb)
Washing soda	Supermarkets and hardware stores	100 g (3¼ oz) per 500 g (1 lb)
Wood-ash lye KOH (Potassium hydroxide)	Make your own.	See recipe.
Lime ($Ca(OH)_2$) (calcium hydroxide)	Papermaking suppliers	30 g (1 oz) in 8 l (16 pt)
Caustic soda (NaOH), sodium hydroxide or lye	Hardware & DIY stores	70 g (2¼ oz) in 8 l (16 pt) of water. Add to small amount of cold water first.

COOKING THE FIBRES

Weighing and cutting fibre

Weigh your fibre when it is dry, then cut it into small pieces – approximately 2.5 cm (1 in.) lengths. If you are using a kitchen blender to do the beating of the fibres (see section on Beating) you may find that the fibres need to be even smaller in length – 1.25 cm (½ in.). If the fibres are any longer they will tangle in the blades.

Soaking

Soak the cut-up fibres overnight to enable them to take up the alkali efficiently.

Cooking equipment

When cooking with alkalis always use a stainless-steel container lest you cause an adverse chemical reaction. Measure out your cooking water at the ratio of about 8 litres (2 gallons) for every pound (500 g) of fibre. You will

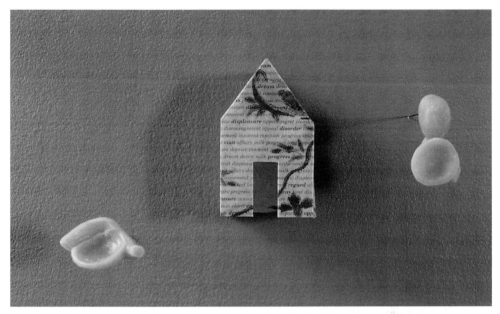

Roberley Bell, *Always the Immigrant*, 1998. Wall installation, detail: 7.6 x 7.6 x 12.7 cm (3 x 3 x 5 in.). Screenprint on handmade flax paper, text and beeswax.

soon be able to judge amounts without measuring every time. Adjust quantities down if you have less fibre.

Making up the alkali

Measure your alkali according to the chart above and add it to the measured water in the pan as it begins to heat up. Check the pH of the solution – around 11 is best.

Adding the fibre

Add the fibre as the water begins to come to the boil. Add more water to cover the fibre if needed.

Testing the fibre

Stir the fibre from time to time. Wearing gloves, test to see if it is done by carefully fishing a small amount of fibre out of the liquid and seeing if you can gently pull it apart. You will be able to see that the fibres begin to look soft as they cook and are thus more likely to be ready.

Rinsing the fibre

Line a sieve or colander with curtain muslin or similar material. Carefully tip your cooked pulp into the lined sieve and rinse under the tap until you have reached 7.5 to 8 on the pH scale. You will see the rinsed-off liquid become clearer and clearer. At the beginning it will have been a dark brown from all the cooked-off unwanted elements of the plant. This rinsing may take anything from a quarter to half an hour. As the indicator strips are expensive, only test the water for pH when you can see a definite improvement in the clarity of the run-off.

The following method applies to all types of fibres cooked. Pour the cooking liquid into a container and test it for pH. If need be, add vinegar until the pH is neutral (7) and dispose of it down the sink. Then rinse the fibres in their sieve under running water until they reach almost neutral. Test the pH from time to time. It is sometimes recommended that paper is left at about 8 on the pH scale to allow for the inevitable slide towards acidity as the paper ages. A little alkalinity will provide a buffer.

PREPARING PULP FROM RAGS

Maureen Richardson, the well-known British papermaker, has granted permission to quote the following extract from her booklet *Plant Papers*.

Rag paper

Natural fibres such as cotton and linen have up to 80% cellulose and will make very good paper. In the paper trade rags are no longer used. Instead, they use cotton linters, which come into the paper mills in the form of boards ready to be broken up. Long-lasting linen papers are used for banknotes and important documents. By using rags to make pulp we are recycling the cotton and linen in the same way we did paper – we have to tear into small pieces – but we do need the aid of chemicals to break down the fibres before liquidising them, because they are much tougher than the recycled paper from wood pulp, which softens by soaking.

Cotton is easier to come by – old sheets or shirts. Do look for labels saying "100% cotton", as unsuitable manmade fibres are often put with cotton to effect quick drying, etc. Old linen tea towels are the easiest way to obtain linen. Tray cloths, tablecloths and serviettes were made in linen – but it is hard to tell pure linen unless it is marked. Worn articles which tear easily are best.

Preparing the rags for pulping

Tear into strips 1 inch wide and cut these strips into squares. Put two quarts of cold water into a clean stainless-steel bucket (or container) and add four tablespoonfuls of caustic soda. Stir until dissolved (use rubber gloves and a wooden spoon), [then] add the squares of cotton or linen. If a white paper is required, keep to the white rags. Some colour, as in printed tea towels, will result in an off-white pulp.

Stir the rag squares into the caustic solution and add warm water to cover them. Stir several times as it comes to the boil, [then] set to simmer. Breaking down the squares will take six to eight hours. A pressure cooker may be used at 18 lbs pressure for two hours for the same result. It saves time, but the cooker cannot then be used for food.

The mixture in the container will turn a dark brown, but the colour will wash out. After thorough washing, small amounts of the rag mixture are added to water in the liquidiser goblet (half the amount of rag that you would have put [into] recycled paper). Liquidising takes two or three times as long also. Use many short bursts until the squares are no longer discernible.

An aid to breaking down stubborn cloth is prolonged soaking in enzymes (obtainable as laundry powders for stain removal). Make up a strong solution and leave torn-up cotton or linen squares in a lidded glass or plastic container for several weeks. Wash away the jelly-like liquid and process the rags in the liquidiser. Test to see if the squares will part easily when torn.

A soft paper can be made by putting 1 inch torn squares of uncooked rags in the coffee grinder to break them down, then in the liquidiser to make a pulp.

OTHER ADDITIVES USED IN PAPERMAKING

Sizing

Size is a non-cellulose material which renders a paper more resistant to water. Without the addition of this chemical additive, paper pigments can seep into non-printed areas of the image, creating a bleed; water from ink or paint soaks into the paper as if it were a blotter. Gelatin sizing is a surface sizing of animal glue or gelatin.

The size can be applied in two different ways: if you are using a Hollander beater, it can either be mixed into paper fibre in its wet state at the end of the beating cycle, a method referred to as internal sizing; or it can be coated onto the finished, dry paper sheet, a method referred to as gelatin, tub or surface sizing. Surface sizing coats the paper, rendering a sturdier finish than that of internal sizing, and gelatin sizing strengthens a sheet made from short fibres.

Nowadays, vegetable starches such as wheat, rice or potato starch, as well as gelatin and gum arabic, can be used to surface-size paper, while polyvinyl emulsions, e.g. methylcellulose (which can be purchased from papermaking suppliers – see list of suppliers), have water-resistant charac-teristics and can strengthen paper made from short fibres.

If you are using a hand blender to process pulp, add the sizing, accord-ing to the manufacturer's instructions, to your entire batch of pulp once it is immersed in water.

An internal sizing agent which performs well is Aquapel, a synthetic material used for internal sizing that is readily available from commercial paper mills.

Calcium carbonate ($CaCO_3$)

This is a form of limestone or precipitated chalk that when added to pulp serves as a buffering agent to protect against acidity. Used extensively in alkaline papers, it adds opacity to the sheet.

Kaolin (china clay)

Fillers such as Kaolin improve the surface opacity and smoothness of the sheet. It is also often used in the making of paper sculpture.

Titanium dioxide

This filler is a pigment used to make a whiter, more opaque paper. It gives a smoother surface to the paper, rendering it less prone to 'picking' during printing.

Retention agent

This is a resinous, cationic liquid available in powder or liquid form, which when added to wet pulp along with pigment ensures that both bond, that colour is retained and that no 'bleeding out' occurs.

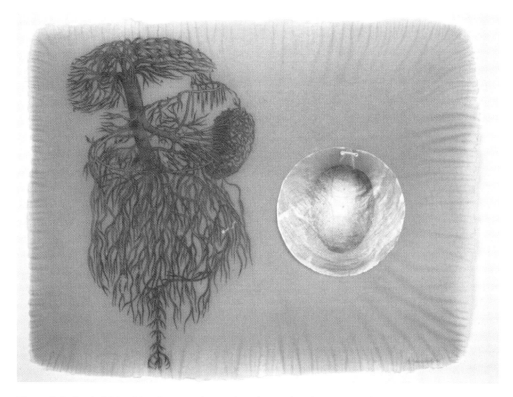

Eileen Foti; *Earth*, 2001, 28 x 21.5 cm (11 x 8½ in.). Handmade paper, inclusions, lithography. Courtesy of the artist.

Formation aid

In its natural form, a substance used in Japanese papermaking to slow drainage during sheet-forming, thus improving distribution of fibre in the vat. In Japan, papermakers use natural formation aid, extracted from the root of the plant *tororo-aoi (Hibiscus manihot (L.))*. A mucous substance, referred to as *neri*, is taken from the crushed roots.

Synthetic formation aids are now available through papermaking suppliers in the USA. These include PMP, PNS and PEO. Formation agents can also be made from okra and from the roots of the hollyhock.

Methylcellulose

This is an adhesive available in powder form, which when added to water makes a glue that is both archival and strengthening. This will glue paper to paper in either a dry or wet state.

BEATING

It is necessary to beat the fibres, separating them and making them soft and pliable, before they can be turned into a pulp. Water is then added to turn the pulp into a slurry from which the embryonic sheet of paper can be pulled. The process of beating enables the individual cellulose fibres to be separated out, exposing the little fibrils on the surface of the fibres, thereby providing a larger surface area for bonding. Cellulose is a carbohydrate made of carbon, hydrogen and oxygen, with its hydrogen and oxygen atoms occurring in the same ratio as they do in water. This means that cellulose is hydrophilic, namely that it loves water and absorbs it easily. Beating shortens the fibres, distributing them more evenly and enabling water to penetrate them. A process called hydrogen bonding takes place between the hydrogen atoms of the molecules of water. As the formed sheet is being pressed and dried, the water molecules are removed from between the fibres, allowing the hydrogen atoms in the cellulose molecules to connect and form their own hydrogen bonds. This produces the strength in the paper.

Beating methods

There are various ways of beating paper both by hand and by machine. The original papermakers in the east would have beaten pulp by hand using special beating sticks, mallets or even stones. They went on to develop stamper beaters. As papermaking spread around the world various other mechanical methods were developed (see Early Beginnings chapter).

Hand-beating

To use the hand-beating method, take out a small handful of your cooked and rinsed fibres, squeezing out excess water but still keeping it moist. Place the small heap of fibres on a board or other hard surface. You can beat straight onto a board, or enclose the fibres within a folded sheet of heavy-duty plastic and beat them through the plastic until the fibres become separate. The fibres will spread out as you beat, but keep drawing them back in. This could take about 15 minutes, though the length of time will vary depending on which plant fibre you are using.

Continue to beat, but this time keep adding small amounts of water to the fibres whenever they have absorbed the previous quantity of water, at the same time drawing them in and turning them. Keep pounding for at least another 15 minutes, as they become softer and more pliable, before testing them as follows.

The jam-jar test

Take a clean jam jar with a well-fitting lid. Put in a pinch of the pulp, fill the jar up with water, put the lid on tightly and then shake up the contents. If the fibres are evenly dispersed throughout the water, then the pulp is ready to use. You can use this test for any kind of pulp prepared by any method.

Storage of pulp

If you are going to use the pulp straight away, you can then add it to water in a vat and proceed to make your sheets of paper. Strain off some of the excess water from a quantity of the pulp in order to provide yourself with a reservoir of pulp. Use a sieve lined with curtain muslin to do this, as you can gather up the muslin bag and squeeze the pulp gently through the fabric to speed up the removal of the water without losing any of your precious pulp. Keep the pulp in the reservoir very moist in order that it will mix easily into the vat when needed. If you are not ready to do this, you can store the pulp, drained of water, in an airtight container in the refrigerator until needed. If it is stored for a while it may start to smell, in which case refresh it by putting it in a muslin-lined sieve and running fresh water through it. For long-term storage, pulp can either be well drained and frozen, or it can also be kept in the refrigerator as outlined above for up to three weeks, or if dried it can be kept indefinitely. To dry, squeeze out all the water using the muslin-bag method, or squeeze the pulp, wrapped in a cloth, in the press. If it is not contained in some way when you do this, it can spread all over the place, and you may lose some of your hard-won pulp. Next, dry it completely somewhere warm. Before using the pulp again, no matter how it has been stored, you will have to rehydrate it by briefly blending or hand-beating it. At this stage, a hand-held electric whisk or a mixing attachment for an electric drill can also be used. Bear in mind that each time it is dried out and stored, then taken out to be used again, it will take up less water, which in turn will affect the resulting paper.

Beating with a blender

Hand-beating is obviously a time-consuming way of working, so many artists will use a kitchen blender or liquidiser. These machines are relatively inexpensive to buy but must be used with care to prevent their motors becoming burnt out. Also, be aware that the action of the blender chops rather than fibrillates the fibres; however, it is possible to add a small quantity of hand-beaten pulp to the blended pulp in the vat, which will give your paper more character. When using a blender, keep the ratio of pulp to water low, adding only a handful of pulp to a blender goblet which is three-quarters filled with cold water. Process the pulp by using the blender in short bursts of about 15 seconds, using the jam-jar test to see when it is ready. If you intend to make your sheets of paper immediately, you can add the pulp to your vat, which can be a washing-up bowl or any other suitably sized container. The size will depend on the size of the mould and deckle with which you will make your paper. Too large a vat is not advised as it would take a great deal of pulp to fill.

Making a reservoir of pulp

When making paper you will need a reservoir of pulp with which to top up your vat as you make your sheets. Every time you make a sheet of paper you are taking pulp out of the vat; if it is not replenished, there will be less and less pulp per volume of water as you go on, and the sheets of paper will be become increasingly thin. If you are making sheets of paper for printmaking, you will obviously want to have paper of a consistent thick-ness. With a reservoir of pulp to hand, you can add small quantities to the mixture as you go along.

Hollander beater

One of the best ways of making pulp, especially large quantities, is to use a Hollander beater. This now electrically driven machine was invented in the late 17th century and has been adapted over the years. There are various makes of Hollander beater which, although varying in details, all operate in much the same way. One example is the beater made by Peter Gentenaar in the Netherlands. It consists of a container in the shape of a letter 'O' made of a rust-free metal such as stainless steel, which forms a channel along which the water and pulp are driven. Part-way along one side of the channel is a knife roll consisting of a cylinder with blunt-edged blades attached around its circumference. In this machine the knife roll is mounted to hang and, with the aid of a counterbalancing arm with a sliding weight, is capable of beating very long fibres. This is because the knife roll can be positioned to be light enough to allow the long, possibly tangled fibres to pass under it. When all the fibres have been processed for a while, the knife roll can be lowered and the weight from the counterbal-ance can be adjusted to increase the impact on the fibres. There is a curved bedplate, usually made of bronze, under the knife roll. By varying the

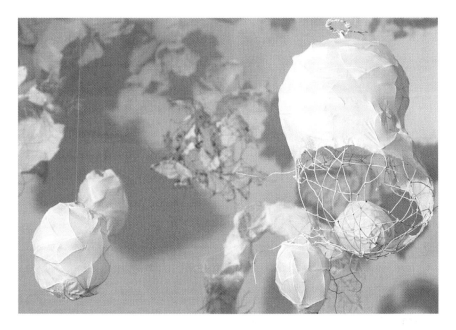

Karen Margolis; *M-Theory* (detail), 2001. Translucent abaca laminated over cotton wire.
Courtesy of Dieu Donné.

distance between the knife roll and the bedplate, you can alter the action
on the fibres. It is possible to control the beating process according to the
kind of paper you want to make, producing pulps with many different
characteristics. These are wonderfully versatile machines, capable of
beating soaked, cut-up, raw fabric, e.g., old denims or old linen sheets, as
well as pre-soaked half-stuff like cotton linters, or prepared plant material.
It is even possible to beat raw flax in it.

Needless to say, these wonderful machines are expensive, but if you
are able to attend a workshop which has one, it would be well worth the
experience.

PREPARING YOUR VAT

You can use any leakproof and rustproof rectangular container as a vat to
hold your pulp, provided it is large enough to comfortably accommodate
your mould and deckle and your hands as you work. Also, you do not want
the vat to be too shallow: there needs to be sufficient space between the
surface of the water and the top of the vat to prevent water splashing out,
and sufficient depth to allow the pulp to come about halfway up the mould
if it is stood on its end in the water.

SHEET-FORMATION METHODS

There are a few methods for forming sheets: the Western method, the Oriental method, and a method using a deckle box. For further advice and for illustrations of sheet forming, see *The Papermaker's Companion* (Helen Hiebert, Storey Publishing, 2000) and *The Art and Craft of Papermaking* (Sophie Dawson, Sterling Publishing, 1999).

Before pulling your first sheet of paper, you must make yourself a work-station where you will couch (as in the French verb *coucher*, which has the meaning 'to lay (something) down') your sheets of paper.

When you come to couch your sheet of paper, you should do it in one smooth rolling action; to facilitate this, many specialist couching tables have a bevelled surface. To mimic this bevel, you can make a pad of some sort, over which you then lay the cloth on which your wet sheet of paper will be laid and upon which it will be carried to be pressed. Traditionally, these cloths would have been felts. Old washed-up woollen blankets can be cut up and used as felts but you can also use (size permitting) a dampened kitchen cloth (a J-cloth or similar). If you need larger felts than allowed by the kitchen cloths, you can use dressmaker's interfacing, sometimes known as Vilene, cut to size. This should be folded into a small pad (you can also use several sheets of newspaper folded into large, medium and small sizes, which go together to make a pad of gradually increasing size), which should then be laid onto a firm, preferably waterproofed board lying on your working surface. Then lay a second cloth, also damp, over the pad. You can, if you wish, spread an old blanket or some old newspapers across your worktable before setting down the board with the pad on it. This will help to mop up any excess water that occurs. Keep your working area clean and, if working with more than one type of pulp, do not cross-contaminate them. Keep the edges of your vats and moulds and deckles clean of scraps of pulp, which adhere and dry on, lest they get into your vat and spoil your pulp.

Western method

The ratio of pulp to water is dependent upon how thick you want your sheets of paper to be; you will learn from experience how much pulp you need to add. The easiest way to check whether the ratio is correct is to pull a sheet, couch and press it. If it is not thick enough add more pulp, and if it is too thick remove some pulp with a sieve.

1. Firstly, stir the pulp in the vat. Left to its own devices the pulp settles to the bottom of the vat, whereas it needs to be evenly dispersed throughout. Do this every time you are about to make a sheet.

2. Remember that cellulose is hydrophilic; therefore, before pulling your first sheet, you should always wet your mould and deckle by laying it against the surface of the liquid in the vat. This is also why the cloths on your couching place should be damp.

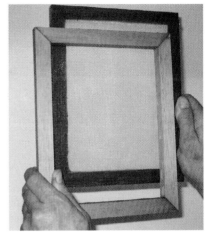

Fig. 1

3. Place the deckle on top of the mould with the mesh side uppermost. Hold it with your thumbs on the top, shorter sides and your fingers underneath. Be careful to keep your fingers and thumbs touching only the wood and never the mesh, as this will cause thinner pieces or even holes in the wet sheet. (*Fig.1*)

4. Holding the mould and deckle vertically in front of you, stretch out towards the side of the vat farthest away from you and lower the mould and deckle into the pulp, bringing the bottom edge of the deckle towards you until it is horizontal. (*Fig.2*) Then, keeping it horizontal, bring it smoothly to the surface. This should always be performed in one smooth movement. If you do not keep mould and deckle level when bringing it up through the pulp then the sheet of paper will be thicker in one place than another. As you come through the surface of the pulp and the sheet (for a sheet of paper is what it now is for the first time) starts to drain, give the mould a gentle shake from side to side and then from back to front. (*Fig.3*)

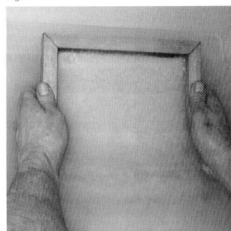

Fig. 2

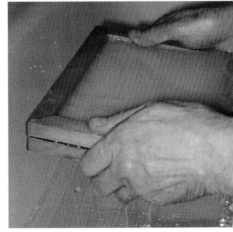

Fig. 3

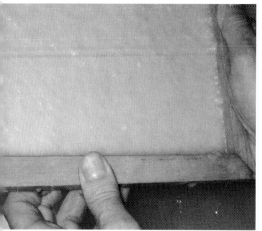

Fig. 4

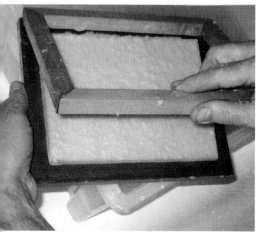

Fig. 5

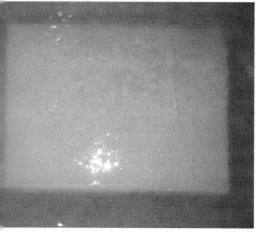

Fig. 6

5. Keep your mould held still above the vat as it drains – you can rest a corner of the mould on the edge of the vat if you wish. (*Fig. 4*)

6. Once it has stopped dripping, you can carefully lift the deckle off the mould. (*Fig. 5*)
Watch lest any water drips off the deckle onto the wet paper surface, because this will make a literal watermark in your paper, known as 'vatman's tears'. Also, be careful not to tilt your mould before the sheet has drained properly, or else the wet sheet may start to slither off the mould.

7. Should your sheet of paper not be perfect, turn over the surface of the mould, touching it and the sheet of paper against the surface of the vat, where the surface tension of the water will pull the sheet of paper back into the mixture: this is called 'kissing it off'. (*Fig. 6*) Stir the contents of the vat again and pull another sheet.

8. To couch your sheet of wet paper, carry your mould with its wet sheet to your couching place. Position the mould vertically on its longest edge on your couching cloth (*Fig. 7*), and in one continuous rolling movement roll the mould and its paper down onto the cloth. This will ensure the surface of the paper continues to touch the cloth as it is rolled down; otherwise air bubbles can become trapped between the sheet of paper and the cloth.

9. Lay a fresh cloth on top of the wet sheet. There is no need to dampen this cloth, as it will become damp from the wet sheet of paper on which it is laid. You may find it helpful to give yourself a registration mark so that you know where to position the mould in order that subsequent sheets can be laid on top of the ones underneath. (*Fig. 8*) Simply place two pieces of tape on either side of where the edge of the mould is positioned, and line it up on subsequent couchings.

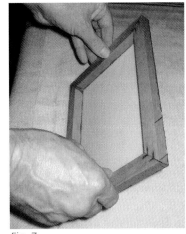

Fig. 7

10. Lay a dry cloth over the final sheet of paper when you are ready to press the sheets. You must then remove the pad you made to give yourself the bevelled surface, as leaving it in during pressing would damage the paper. Place a second waterproofed board on top of the pile, place one hand firmly on top of this board with your other hand underneath the bottom board, and turn the whole 'sandwich' over. Then lift off the board that was formerly on the bottom, remove the pad and replace the board. This pile can now be pressed.

11. You can, of course, press one sheet at a time if you wish. There are various ways of pressing the newly made sheets of paper, for which see below.

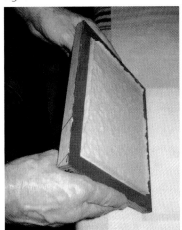

Fig. 8

If you find you have difficulty in couching your sheet of paper, you may be using too dry a felt. Use water to help you release the sheet by gently wiping with a wet sponge across the back of the mesh. Sometimes, if you press down especially firmly on the mould along the leading edge of the paper, that will be enough to free it.

Oriental sheet-forming

This is very different from the Western method since sheets are formed by multiple dippings in the vat, building up several thin layers of fibres. This technique of 'laminating' creates very strong, yet fine papers. It is especially useful with native-plant pulps, especially long-fibred ones; the shorter-fibred pulps, such as cotton linters, are more suited to the one-pull Western method.

The Japanese technique is called *nagashi-zuki* and employs a mucilaginous substance called *neri*, obtained from the root of the *tororo-aoi (Hibiscus manihot (L.))* plant, to help with the formation of sheets. Because of its viscosity, the drainage of the water through the mesh of the *su* (the flexible bamboo mould used in Japan) is slowed

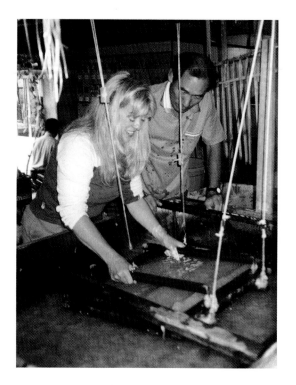

Nagashi-zuki sheet-forming in Japan with master papermaker Okuda-san

down, enabling the longer fibres used in Japanese papermaking to be manipulated without becoming entangled. The *su* is held in a hinged frame, a *keta*. Together the two pieces are referred to as a *sugeta*.

Other plants produce a similar substance to the hibiscus root, e.g., okra. It is also possible to obtain a synthetic formation aid that comes in powder form. This is also very easily made up by sprinkling half a teaspoonful into a liquidiser or blender three quarters full of water whilst the motor is running. Put the cap on the blender but then remove the small round lid in the middle of the larger cap. Five seconds is sufficient to mix it thoroughly, or if you feel it is too thick, add more water. Then store as a stock solution. Note, however, that its shelf life is limited once made up, and in two to three weeks it will be ineffective. This synthetic formation aid is available from Carriage House Paper and comes with clear instructions for use.

There is no hard and fast rule about the amount of formation aid you should use with your pulp. The more you add, the slower will be the drainage, thus enabling you to make very thin sheets. On the other hand, too much formation aid will prevent the fibres from forming a sheet of paper at all. Experience will determine the right amount.

The first dip in the vat is quickly performed and serves only to make a foundation on the *su*. Dip your *sugeta* into the pulp as you would to form a sheet by the Western method, but do not let the back edge of the frame go into the vat. As you come through the surface tilt it away from you and throw off the excess water – this is known as 'throwing the wave'. You will see a scarcely visible film on the *su*. This manoeuvre will come with practice. After a second dipping, gently rock the pulp backwards and forwards across the *su* before throwing off the excess water again. With subsequent dippings alternate the rockings, from side to side then back and forth. Keep dipping until you achieve the desired thickness of paper.

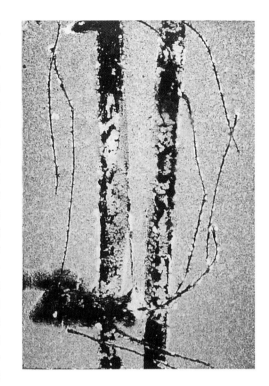

Nancy Manter; *Carved Snow no.3*; 63.5 x 89 cm (25 x 35 in.); handmade paper.

Because the *su* is independent of its frame, you can simply lift the flexible *su* with its sheet of paper on top of it and roll it easily down onto your couching cloth. The *su* should peel away from the paper after it is laid on the couching cloth; if you experience any difficulty, you can apply a little gentle pressure along the edge of the *su*.

Every time you add fresh pulp to the vat, add more formation aid. Traditionally, the Japanese would not lay cloths between each sheet as the paper was made, even when pressing, as the formation aid would be enough to prevent them sticking together; but, if you wish to err on the side of caution, you can use Vilene between each layer.

For further information, refer to the section on the *nagashi-zuki* method, the contemporary Japanese process for making paper, in the Early Beginnings chapter. See also, for clear guidance on the technique of Oriental sheet-forming, Donald Farnsworth's *A Guide to Japanese Papermaking* and Helen Hiebert's *Papermaking with Plants*.

Using a Deckle Box

A deckle box is an adaptation of the Nepalese method of papermaking whereby the mould and deckle is floated in a small pool of water and the pulp is poured in. With a little judicious agitation of the mould the fibres are aligned and the sheet is made. The sheet is usually left to dry on the mould. (You can, of course, use this option with either Western or Japanese methods, as it is especially useful with thin sheets, which should peel off easily when the paper is dry.)

You can make your own deckle box by making an extra deep deckle to fit the size of your mould. However, make sure that your hand can strad-dle the distance when you are holding the deckle together with the mould. The following technique is especially useful when you have only a little pulp to use.

Fill your vat with water, which should come above your mould and into the deckle box when they are floated on the water. Find a container that will hold sufficient paper to make a sheet of paper in one go (this may take some experimenting to get right), and slip it into the water inside the deckle. Holding the deckle, move it and the mould around to agitate the pulp as you would a normal sheet. When the fibres are aligned, raise the mould and deckle from the water and drain. You can leave the sheet on the mould to dry, or you can couch it as in the Western method.

You can, of course, make the mould and deckle any size you wish.

PRESSING

After the sheet of paper has been formed on the mould, the paper needs to be pressed, which removes excess water from the sheets, helping the hydrogen bonding of the cellulose fibres to take place. This also helps to speed the drying process and prevent cockling of the paper. The surface of the finished sheet of paper will also be affected by the texture of whatever kind of felt you use against the wet sheet of paper while it is in the press. Pressing can be done in various ways, from the simple to the sophisticated, according to the equipment you have available.

Leaving on the mould to dry

You can leave your sheet of paper on the mould to dry. Given that the air can circulate well around the mould, the sheet of paper will dry quite quickly, especially if left in a warm place. This is quite a useful method,

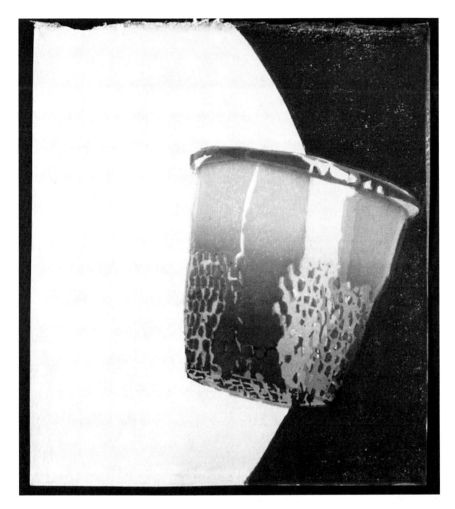

Elspeth Lamb; *Shuttle*, Japanese woodblock print on handmade *kozo* paper, 33 x 28 cm (13 x 11 in.), 2000.

especially if you feel your sheet of paper is of a particularly delicate nature. The drawback to this method is, of course, that you are unable to use your mould again until the sheet of paper has dried.

Sponge press

There are various ways of doing this. One method is to leave your newly made sheet of paper on the mould. Having carefully removed the deckle, lay a clean, dry, absorbent cloth over it and then press gently through it, gradually increasing the pressure. You can then continue to dry and press it by using the ironing method detailed below or, alternatively, transfer it to a sheet of Perspex. For this technique, please refer to the later section on Drying.

Another option is to couch the wet sheet onto a felt laid on a board. Lay a clean, absorbent cloth over the wet sheet, then apply gentle downward pressure with your sponge. Keep wringing out your sponge. Laying a thick wad of newspaper under your board will help to mop up any excess water there may be.

Using an iron

Couch your sheet of paper onto a cloth laid on a thick felt or old blanket, and lay a dry cloth over the wet sheet. Iron the cloth with a hot, dry (non-steam) iron. Pick up the whole 'sandwich' of base cloth (not the thick felt), wet sheet and top felt/cloth, then flip the whole lot over and remove the wet sheet which was formerly on the underside. Replace with a fresh, dry cloth and continue ironing and topping and tailing until the paper is dry, or nearly dry.

Clamps and boards

This simple method of pressing uses G-clamps and boards. It is essential to use strong, thick wooden marine-ply boards – say, about 6-ply thick – which will not warp and will have already been protected by polyurethane varnish. This board must be several inches bigger than the size of the sheets of paper. Depending on the size of the boards, use two (or more) G-clamps evenly spaced down either side, or, like a flower press, you could drill holes in each corner and use wing nuts and screws to hold the whole thing together. Instead of G-clamps, you could use two stout battens laid lengthways along the boards (but longer than them), drilling holes in the ends of the battens, which you then tighten with carriage bolts, nuts and washers. Whichever method you use, take the pressure down gradually. Leave the pile, or 'post' as it is properly called, under pressure for approximately 30 minutes. Then carefully separate each sheet from its neighbour.

Recycled equipment, e.g. book presses

Old-fashioned book presses can be used provided you place protective pressing boards either side of each sheet of paper. You can make these boards from simple hardboard rectangles protected with waterproof varnish. If you are using hardboard, remember that only one side is smooth. This is the side to place against the paper. Put a smooth cloth on either side of the sheet of paper and then sandwich with two pieces of hardboard. Take the pressure up until you can feel the press touching the boards, then wind it up another turn or two until you see the water coming out. Remember that too much pressure can damage your paper and tear it.

Hydraulic press

Presses can be made using recycled car jacks or can be bought ready-made. See the list of suppliers at the end of the book for other books on this subject. A hydraulic press is a very useful piece of equipment if you make a lot of paper, and is easily capable of pressing large posts of paper. Papermaking studios which provide facilities for artists to come in and do their own work will very likely have a hydraulic press.

Vacuum table

A vacuum table is a very versatile piece of equipment which can be used for several different papermaking techniques, one of which is to facilitate the making of very large sheets of paper. Available vacuum systems work on the same principle of atmospheric pressure compressing the wet pulp and causing water to be forced out of it. Some consist of a table with holes drilled in the bed. The holes are connected to plastic pipes which lead to a spherical collecting tank with a one-way valve, which in turn is connected to a vacuum pump. The system must be airtight to function correctly. A large plastic sheet is used to cover the wet pulp in a way that creates a seal over the work and the table, allowing the vacuum to be created. When the vacuum pump is switched on, the air is extracted from the system, allowing atmospheric pressure to squeeze the wet pulp, expelling the water into the collecting tank. About 75% of the water will be removed.

Wet-and-dry vacuum system

This ingenious and well-known idea for papermakers has been widely adapted by many different artists. When your sheet of wet paper is lying on the mould, well-drained and with the deckle removed, take a wet-and-dry vacuum cleaner and use the nozzle against the back of the mesh of the mould, running it up and down to extract as much water as possible. Then either leave your paper to dry on the mould or follow one of the techniques below.

DRYING TECHNIQUES

Air-drying

When you couch your paper onto a thin cloth like a J-cloth or Vilene, you can then peg on a clothes line after pressing. You may find that the paper cockles (warps) if it dries too quickly if exposed to wind or sun, so it may be better to dry it indoors. Allowing the air to circulate around the paper ensures it will dry more quickly than if the felts are laid flat on newspaper.

Restraint-drying

After pressing your paper, you can finish the drying by applying your paper to a sheet of sealed board, glass or Perspex, where it will dry flat under restraint. Some people advise using melamine or Formica, although it might be advisable to lightly oil the surface to ensure the sheet of paper comes off cleanly.

In India, damp sheets of paper are often brushed onto the plaster walls of houses, where they will obviously dry quickly in the heat of the sun. In Japan, traditionally they were brushed onto seasoned boards and left in the sun or, as nowadays, brushed onto the back of a heated metal sheet

Applying paper to a vertical surface of Perspex or glass

1. With a damp cloth lightly moisten the surface of the Perspex or glass.
2. Pick up the felt with the pressed sheet of paper still attached and lay it against the surface of your choice.
3. Carefully hold the cloth with one hand, whilst with the other use either a roller, a brush or a cloth folded into a pad.
4. Gently roll the cloth onto the drying surface, paying particular attention to the edges of the paper, which should be obvious through the cloth.
5. Remember that you only need gentle pressure lest you damage your sheet of paper.
6. To remove the cloth, carefully peel it back to reveal the top edge of the sheet of paper. If any of this edge still adheres to the cloth and has not been transferred to the drying surface, carefully use the back of a fingernail to free the top edge of the paper. Once this edge is against the Perspex, gently lay the cloth back against it and re-roll. You should find that the paper will have been released. Holding the damp cloth in both hands, allow it almost to come off under its own weight.

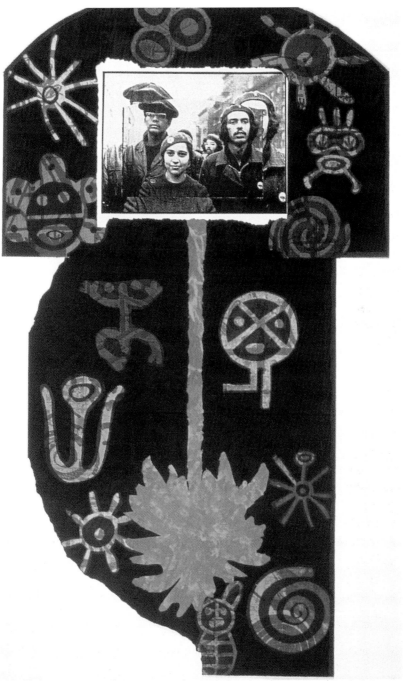

Juan Sanchez; *Once we were warriors*. Lithograph, handmade paper, pulp painting courtesy of RCIPP. Collaborating papermaker: Gail Deery.
Collaborating printer: Randy Hemminghaus

Applying paper to a horizontal surface

1. Lay the sheet of paper complete with its felt flat on the drying surface, which you will first have wiped over with a damp cloth.
2. Roll gently over the back of the cloth.
3. Carefully check that the cloth will free itself from the sheet of paper, using your fingernail as above if any of it still adheres, then remove the cloth completely.

Depending on the ambient temperature, your paper should dry overnight. It will dry flat, with the side that has been against the Perspex being shiny and smooth.

If you experience any difficulty in releasing your sheet of paper, carefully try to free a corner – with the point of a fine blade if necessary. Once you have lifted one corner, carefully free along that edge to the neighbouring corner, then, using both hands, gently pull the paper off the drying surface.

In extreme cases, you may need to lay a damp cloth gently against the back of the dried sheet of paper or very lightly mist it with some water from a spray bottle before it will come away. Occasionally, a sheet of paper may spring off the drying surface. If so you should flatten it by placing it under pressure for a short while. If necessary, if it has cockled, you can lightly spray the sheet with water and iron it flat.

Leaving your sheet of paper on the mould to dry

This is self-explanatory and has already been referred to earlier in the text.
1. Leave your sheet of paper on its mould and lay your mould with one end propped up on some sort of small wedge, allowing the air to circulate around the mould.
2. When the top of the sheet of paper begins to dry, turn the mould around.
3. To release the paper, carefully apply the point of a sharp knife or blade to one corner of the paper and prise it up, slipping the blade gently along just under the top edge of the paper. It should come away easily.
4. You will notice that the two surfaces of the paper are of different textures, with one bearing the impression of the mesh of the mould.

Exchange-drying

When drying a post of papers, you can exchange-dry the sheets. Rather like the topping and tailing of cloths detailed in the section on using an iron to dry and press the paper, exchange-drying involves using fresh, dry

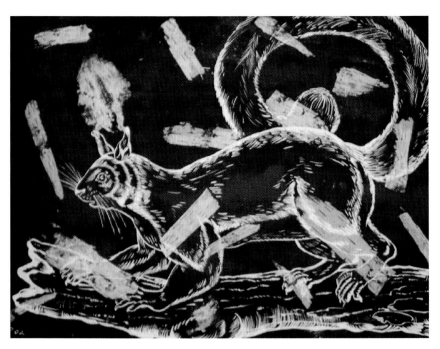

Ken Polinskie, *Out on a Limb*, 2003; 47 x 71 cm (18½ x 28 in.). Print on handmade (linen/cotton) paper with birch-bark inclusions.

absorbent cloths, felts or sheets of acid-free blotting paper to interleave your sheets of freshly-pressed paper so as to draw the moisture out, before placing them back under pressure for several hours. Thereafter, keep exchanging the felts or blotters between the sheets of paper, returning the pile to the press under lighter pressure than before until your paper is dry.

Sophie Dawson in *The Art and Craft of Papermaking* recommends placing felts on just the top and bottom of the pile rather than interleaving one with every sheet. She does suggest, however, that you should separate and restack the papers, rearranging them each time you replace the top and bottom felts until the paper is dry and smooth.

As a final step you can interleave your now-dry sheets of paper with smooth, acid-free mount board and leave under pressure for an hour, which will smooth your sheets of paper.

This last pressing process is called 'calendering'. The same effect can also be achieved by running sheets of paper through the etching press against a clean, smooth copperplate or similar. Commercially made papers that have been run through hot rollers or plates are called 'hot-pressed'. If you have dried your paper on Perspex or glass, the finish will be similar to hot-pressed paper.

3 · MAKING A SIMPLE WESTERN-STYLE MOULD AND DECKLE

A sheet of paper is formed on a mould. The deckle is a simple frame which is the same size as the mould and sits on top of it. The deckle determines the size and depth of the sheet, producing sheets of paper whose edges have an interesting 'feathered' appearance. Printmakers will be familiar with this deckle edge, which is evident on quality printing papers. Of course, some papermaking suppliers stock beautifully crafted moulds and deckles, but you'll need to be prepared to pay for this service (see List of Suppliers).

Moulds come in various types: the Western mould and deckle, the Japanese *sugeta* and the deckle box. (See the section on moulds and deckles in the Early Beginnings chapter, and the section on sheet-formation methods in the Setting Up chapter. *The Art and Craft of Papermaking* by Sophie Dawson, *Papermaking* by Jules Heller and *The Papermaker's Companion* by Helen Hiebert also have detailed instructions on how to make moulds and deckles – see Bibliography.)

A simple mould and deckle can be constructed using ¾ x ¾-inch pine, brass or decking screws and waterproof glue, all available from hardware stores.

The joints are simply constructed by butt jointing. That is, the joint is made purely by lapping the longer piece of wood over the end of the shorter piece, drilling through this outer piece of wood into the end grain of the shorter piece, and then screwing through the wood using rustproof screws (for example, brass or decking screws). The process breaks down into the following steps:

1. Decide on the size of the paper you want to make.
2. Cut two pieces of wood which are exactly the same length as the width of the desired piece of paper plus 4 cm (1½ in).
3. Butt-joint one of the shorter pieces with one of the longer pieces, forming a right angle.
4. Hold these two bits of wood in position with two clamps.

5. Drill through the longer piece of wood into the end grain of the shorter piece, using a drill bit that is appropriate for the screws you intend to use.

6. Countersink the hole drilled by using a countersink drill bit.

7. Loosen one of your clamps.

8. Apply waterproof glue (easily obtainable at any hardware store) to the end grain of the shorter piece of wood

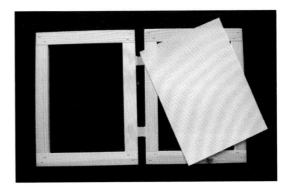

A hinged frame.

9. Reposition your pieces of wood and reclamp.

10. Screw the pieces of wood together using a rustproof screw (brass or decking screws, again easily obtainable at any hardware store).

11. Repeat the process for the other three joints.

12. Repeat this procedure for the deckle.

13. Apply a coat of polyurethane varnish to both mould and deckle. Allow to dry overnight, then reapply.

14. If the longer side of the mould

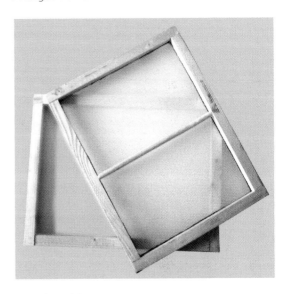

A reinforced frame.

is bigger than approximately 25 cm (10 in.), then a cross-strut should be inserted halfway down the length of the wood in such a way that it does not touch the mesh that will later be attached, as this will spoil your sheets of paper.

15. Apply the mesh. Note that for best results, have it applied by companies that deal with screenprinting equipment, such as Sericol (see List of Suppliers), as they will achieve a tautness of mesh unobtainable any other way. Such tautness enables easier couching of the wet sheet. A mesh size of 10 tpi (threads per inch) is good, but ask their advice. It is very important when the glue is applied by these firms that they do not allow it to go over the edge of the wood onto the mesh, as this will block holes, thus interfering with the quality of the sheet.

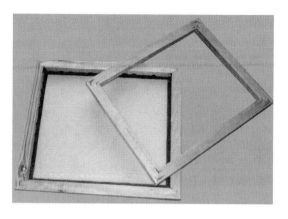

A simple frame.

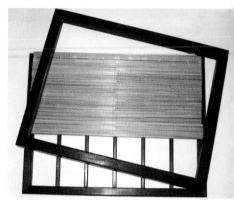

A Japanese *sugeta* and *su.*

16. Polyester mesh or brass screening may be acquired from papermaking suppliers like Carriage House Paper and Lee Scott McDonald in the USA, or from some local hardware shops (get 30 to 40 wires per inch). Polyester mesh should be cut to the same size as the mould, and can be stapled round the frame close to the outside edge. Waterproof adhesive tape should then be applied on top of the tacks or staples round the edge of the screen, so that pulp will not be caught under the screen mesh.

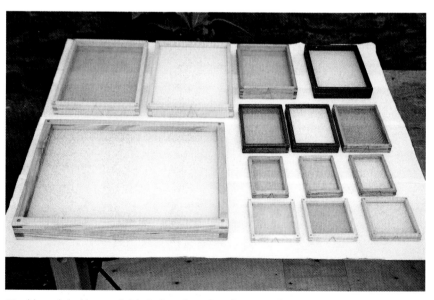

Moulds and deckles available to buy (see *Suppliers* p.141).

4 · PULP PAINTING

by Eileen Foti

Pulp painting is a diverse and creative technique that allows an artist to manipulate overbeaten pigmented pulp on top of a wet base sheet in a variety of ways, creating marks and textures reminiscent of certain painting styles, yet maintaining characteristics true to paper. Helen Frederick's *Clean Air, Clear Sky* (page 59) is a rich example, created by brushing layer upon layer of pigmented linen on top of a linen base sheet. A pulp painting can be made to stand on its own as a complete image; it can be combined with other papermaking techniques; or it can be made to register to various printmaking matrices, creating a comfortable relationship between print and paper. This chapter will explore basic techniques of pulp painting, with special consideration for artists interested in combining those methods with printed information.

FIBRE PREPARATION

Beating

There are certain advantages to using overbeaten pulp as the pulp paint. Whether using cotton, linen, abaca or flax, the more finely it is beaten, the easier it will be to manipulate with a brush, squeeze bottle, or syringe. Usually, pulp for painting is mechanically beaten for four to eight hours, depending on the type of fibre. In addition to being easier to manipulate, overbeaten pulp can attain a higher level of colour saturation when being pigmented, because there are so many abrasions on the surface of each fibre due to the beater's macerating action, providing more areas to which the colour can attach itself. Of course, you can paint with pulps beaten for less time, but they may not be as fluid even when using additives, or you can experiment with the ratio of fibre to water (see below: Pulp Painting and Stencilling Techniques). Pulp that is not overbeaten can have a more fibrous and sometimes clumpy look, because the individual strands are longer, whereas with overbeaten pulp each single, minuscule fibre becomes more anonymous, allowing a full range of tonal shades, washes and rich solids. Overbeaten pulp will also form cleaner edges when applied through a stencil.

How to select and prepare the fibre for base sheets to be pulp-painted is determined by several factors, such as the type of fibre desired, opacity versus translucency, the colour, rate of shrinkage, absorbency, weight, etc. In addition to the obvious aesthetic concerns, a printmaker must also consider what type of base sheet will work best with whichever print technique he or she is planning to use.

Pigmenting pulp

After pulps for base sheets and paints have been beaten, they are ready to be coloured. Papermakers can use different types of pigments or dyes. Aqueous dispersed pigments are a safer alternative to dry pigments or dyes, which can be toxic and/or not truly lightfast. Unlike dyes, aqueous dispersed pigments do not penetrate into the fibres; instead, they cling to the outer surface of each fibre, and require an additive called retention agent to facilitate that bonding process. Aqueous dispersed pigments can be purchased from several papermaking supply companies, and each will include a set of directions for their product. Some will suggest using the retention agent (or retention aid) before adding the pigment, and some will suggest adding it after. It is important to dilute the retention agent in a cup of water and mix it into the pulp for at least ten minutes, either manually, with a whiz mixer, or in the beater. When using highly saturated pigments, it may be wise to let pulp sit for a few hours, or even overnight, after adding the retention agent. It is a good idea to strain the liquid pigments through a fine mesh before adding them, to make sure that any dry particles from the lid or rim do not fall into the pulp, as these can cause unwanted flecks of colour in the finished sheets. When the pigment is properly retained by the pulp, the water in which the pulp is floating should be clear. Once overbeaten pulps for painting have been pigmented, they can be mixed together like ink or paint to create a wide-ranging palette. For a thorough explanation of pigments and dyes, refer to *Color For the Hand Papermaker* by Elaine Koretsky.

Sizing

Sizing is added to make paper less absorbent. It coats the fibres, making them less permeable to water, ink or paint, so that bleeding or feathering does not occur. This is of great concern for printmakers who would want to dampen and/or print on handmade sheets. In addition to making paper less absorbent and stronger, sizing is also effective in helping protect paper

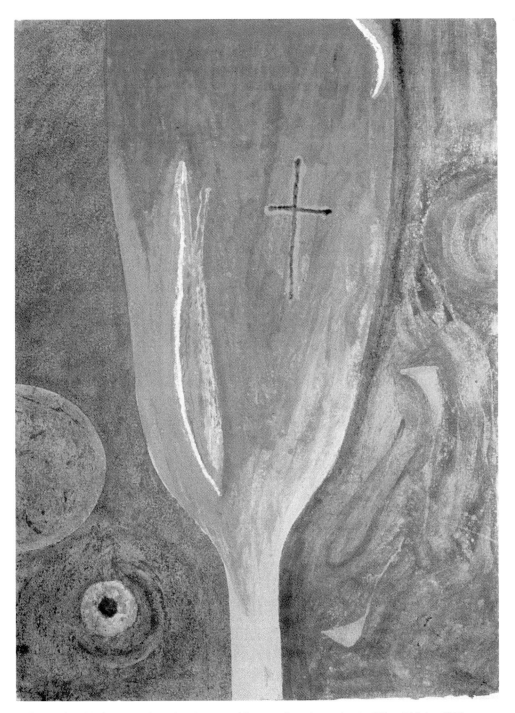

Helen Frederick, *Clean Air, Clear Sky.* Pigmented linen on linen base sheet; 42⅕ x 30⅘ in. 1990. Produced by the artist. Courtesy of the artist.

that is exposed to air and dust, thus prolonging its life. Sizing also hardens the fibres, therefore making it easier for a printer to use tacky ink without worrying about the fibres 'picking' or being pulled out and sticking to the residual ink film on the plate or block, which then would get imported back to the slab during re-inking. This is especially bothersome in plano-graphic and relief printing.

There are two basic methods for sizing paper. Internal sizing coats the individual fibres, but leaves the structure of the paper open enough to accept the printing ink that is forced down into it by the pressure of the press. External sizing all but seals the surface of the sheet, making it more impermeable to types of ink or other fluid media that are meant to sit on the paper's surface.

Internal sizing, an alkyl-ketene-dimer emulsion with a neutral pH, can be added to the pulp during the last few minutes of the beating cycle. It can also be stirred manually into a pail or vat of pulp. (Remember, if you want to use sizing, add it after you have used pigments and retention agents, or else it may seal each fibre, making it difficult for pigments to bond.) Always mix the sizing into a cup of water before pouring it in. The sizing takes a few days to properly develop within the finished sheet of paper. It can also be set with heat. If you are planning to print on sheets that have just been made and you cannot wait a few days for the sizing to set on its own, then iron the sheets on a medium-heat setting. Two commonly used industrial brands of internal sizing are Hercon 70 and Aquapel. Follow the manufacturer's or supplier's directions.

The other method for sizing paper is to do it externally once the newly formed sheets have dried. Also called 'surface sizing', this method provides a heavier size than when using the internal type by itself. For a sturdier finish it is best to use both, since the internal sizing will keep the external sizing from seeping too deeply into the fibres, thus retaining its benefit on the paper's surface. Using internal sizing will also keep the sheet stronger during the process of rewetting it with the surface sizing. Types of external sizing include rabbit-skin glue, methylcellulose, and wheat or rice starches. Another standard sizing is a water/gelatin solution (at the ratio of 40:1), and simple directions for this effective method can be found in *A Papermaker's Companion* by Helen Hiebert. Surface sizing can be applied by dipping the sheets into a shallow tray of solution, or by brushing, spraying or rolling. A commercial product called Surface Size 700 is extremely effective and has a shelf life of about two years. Again, follow manufacturer's or supplier's directions.

PULP PAINTING AND STENCILLING TECHNIQUES

There are several basic techniques that leave the door wide open for innovation and individuality, and with each a wide range of mark-making can be achieved. By following simple registration methods, printmakers can use pulp painting to repetitively lay down colours on newly formed base sheets prior to printing. Pulp can be applied to a base sheet with brushes, squeeze bottles (similar to the ketchup and mustard bottles found in restaurants), syringes and ladles, as well as through a variety of stencils, and can be registered to any printmaking matrix. As with any hand-colouring method, there might be slight variations in some of the pulp-painted areas, but the character and registration will be the same throughout the edition.

Additives

In most cases it is necessary to modify the pulp, making it easier to manipulate when painting with it. Commonly used additives are methylcellulose and formation aid. Each artist must experiment with how much of these additives to use, as the amount is determined by feel and not by calculation.

Methylcellulose is a reversible, archival adhesive that is also invaluable for pulp painting. It makes the pulp easier to manipulate with a brush, similar in feeling to the way a tack reducer makes a stiff printing ink become more fluid. Simply mix methylcellulose into your container of pulp until a desirable painting

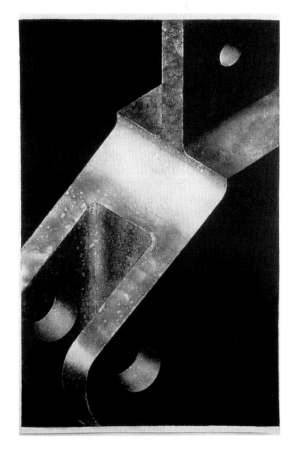

Robert Cottingham, *Component #5*. Linen pulp painting on cotton base sheet, 152.5 x 101.5 cm (60 x 40 in.); 2003. Produced at Dieu Donné Papermill. Collaborating Master Papermaker: Paul Wong. Courtesy of the artist.

consistency is reached. Methylcellulose comes in a powder form. For best results, follow the manufacturer's or supplier's directions.

Formation aid is a deflocculant that keeps fibres from entangling during the sheet-forming process. It makes the water more viscous, which slows down the drainage time. It also helps pulp paint and water to flow more easily through the tip of a squeeze bottle. Experiment with how much formation aid you add and with the water-to-pulp ratio, and make sure to frequently shake the bottle so that the water and pulp don't separate. Formation aid is a synthetic version of the Japanese *tororo-aoi*, the viscous substance extracted from the roots of the *tororo* plant. There are three types. The first is PNS, which should not be mixed into pulp containing any other additives, such as retention aid or sizing; the other two are PEO and PMP. All three are compatible with all other additives, making any one a good choice for pulp painting. They come in a powdered form, so, again, follow the manufacturer's or supplier's directions.

Registration

A pulp painting can certainly be made spontaneously, without the need for registering successive layers or using stencils. However, if needed, the registration key commonly used in printmaking, a fine-line permanent-marker drawing on a Mylar sheet, can be used to register layers or areas of pulp paint to each other or to subsequent printed runs. A separate Mylar sheet (cut to the exact size of the handmade-paper base sheet) for each layer of pulp paint is traced off the key drawing, and only the areas to be painted are then cut away. One by one, each Mylar sheet is placed on top of the newly formed base sheet, and pulp paint is applied to the exposed areas. A tracing of that same key drawing can then be transferred to a printmaking matrix.

Another registration method uses one single sheet of Mylar. Robert Cottingham's *Component #5* (page 61) began with a true-to-scale line drawing on Mylar that was cut to the size of the intended base sheet and delineated all of the contours of the machine's parts. The parts were then cut out individually, like the pieces of a big jigsaw puzzle. Next, a yellow cotton base sheet was formed and the Mylar puzzle was reassembled on top of it. An individual Mylar piece was removed, exposing the base sheet underneath. That section was then filled in with black or grey overbeaten linen pulp dispensed from a squeeze bottle. The gradations were created by carefully spraying water from a fine nozzle into that new pulp layer. Once completed, that section was then covered up again with its corresponding Mylar shape, and the remaining pieces were tackled one by one.

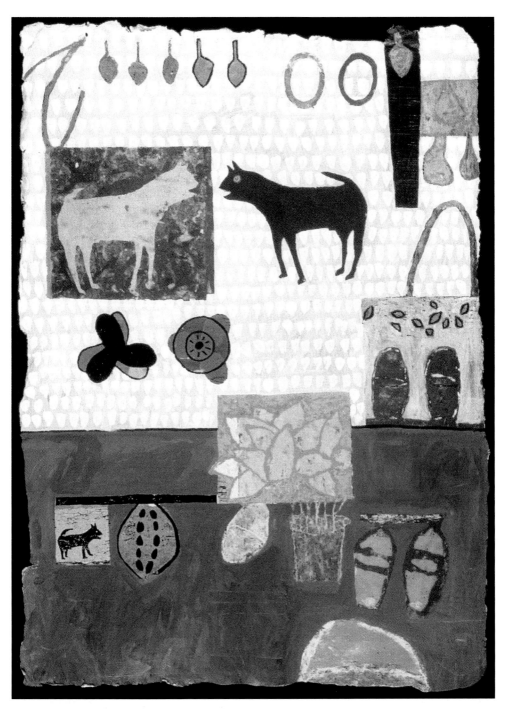

Ellen Hill, *All Over the Map*. Pulp painting, woodcut, and acrylic paint. 76 x 56 cm (30 x 22 in.); 2000. Produced by the artist. Courtesy of the artist.

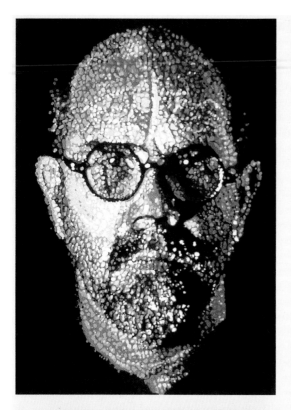

Chuck Close. *Self-Portrait/Pulp.* Coloured linen pulp on white cotton carrier sheet, 146 x 101.5 cm (57½ x 40 in.), 2001. Pace Editions, Inc. Papermakers: Ruth Lingen, Mae Shore, Jacob Lewis.
Dieu Donné Papermill Papermakers: Paul Wong, Matt Jackson, Anne Polashenski. Published by Pace Editions, Inc., courtesy of Pace Editions, Inc.

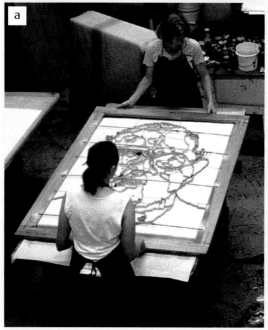

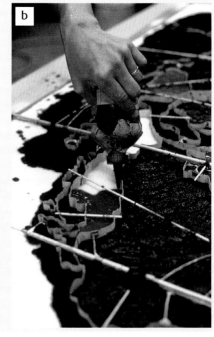

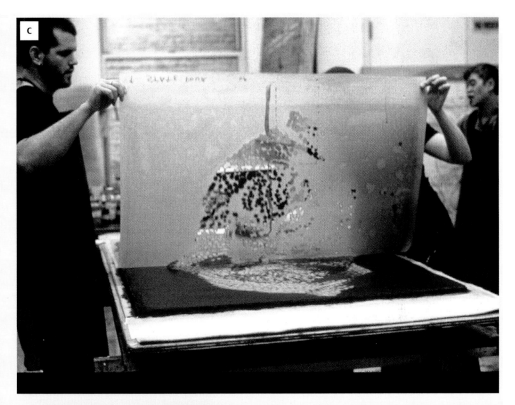

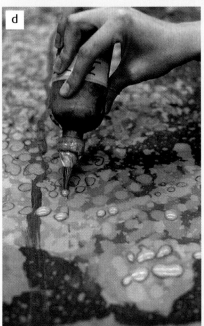

a) The brass shim stencil is placed onto the base sheet.

b) Stencils are filled in with black and grey pulp using squeeze bottles.

c) Lexan stencil is laid down in perfect registration.

d) Pulp is applied through the stencil using squeeze bottles with cake decorating tips.

Photos Courtesy of Pace Editions, Inc.

All Over the Map (p. 63) was first created by Ellen Hill as a straight pulp painting. After it was finished, she decided to add a woodblock print and some hand-colouring, so she put a Mylar over the dry pulp piece and traced a registration key. Hill transferred the information to a woodblock, which enabled her to carve and print a matrix that lined up beautifully with the painting. She finished by hand-colouring with acrylic paint.

Other types of stencils

Stencils can also be hand-cut from pellon (interfacing material used in sewing), thin craft foam sheets, or even recycled x-rays. Found materials such as cookie cutters and plastic fluorescent-lighting grids are great for corralling pulp paint on top of a base sheet. It can be poured in, spooned in or applied with a squeeze bottle. Just leave the stencil form in place until the water from the pulp paint is absorbed into the base sheet, so that it doesn't run or bleed when the stencil is removed.

Chuck Close's incredibly intricate *Self-Portrait/Pulp* (page 64) was made with a brass shim stencil and eight Lexan stencils. The shim stencil was tailor-made from brass cookie-cutter shapes soldered together inside a big wooden frame (a). It was laid down on top of a white cotton base sheet, and, after the grey-and-black-linen background colours were filled in with squeeze bottles (b), the shim was removed. Then each Lexan stencil was laid down (c), and the remaining colours, from dark grey to white, were added (d). The illusion of depth is truly stunning.

Other techniques

Instead of applying pulp paint directly to a base sheet, some artists choose to paint right onto the mould. In *Deep Blue Page V* (opposite) Amanda Guest, working in reverse, dropped and manipulated linen pulp directly onto the surface of the mould, then couched it onto a felt. After building up several layers in this manner, a white watermarked linen sheet and then a final dark-blue/black backer sheet were couched on top (see Watermarks chapter). When pressed, dried and flipped over, the pulp painting sits on top of the white watermarked sheet, which is backed by the dark base sheet.

OPPOSITE Amanda Guest, *Deep Blue Page V*. Pulp painting and watermarked linen on pigmented linen, 41.5 x 63.5 cm (36 x 25 in.); 1999; Produced at Dieu Donné Papermill. Collaborating master papermaker: Paul Wong. Courtesy of the artist.

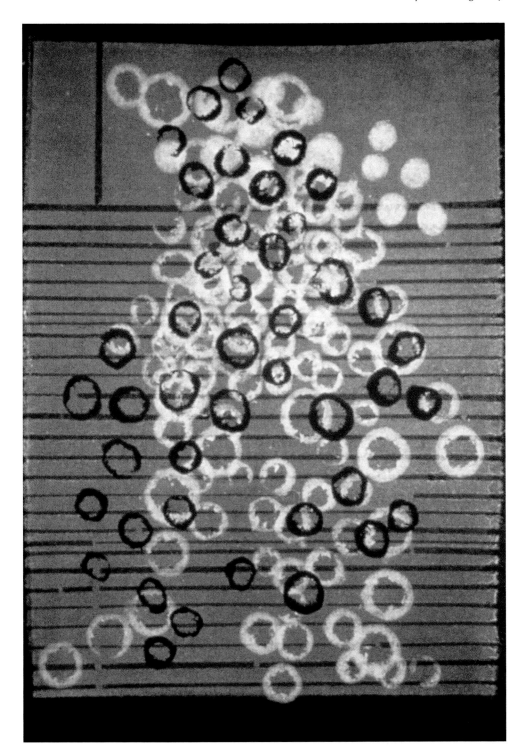

Shannon Brock combines multilayer pulp painting with water-soluble pencil transfers. In her twelve-panel piece, *Poor Kids Have Lawns of Dandelions* (opposite), Brock built up several layers of pigmented cotton: some formed with contact paper blocking out areas on the mould; some formed as veils and then 'drawn' into by squeezing water through a dental syringe before couching; and, finally, some painted with pigmented flax and methylcellulose. Brock then pressed the sheets, using half pressure, in preparation for the transfer. Next, using water-soluble pencils such as Rexel Derwents, she drew backwards on translucent pellon. (An image can be drawn on pellon with a permanent marker in the same way that printmakers use Mylar. It is then turned over and the pencil drawing is made.) She then dropped the pellon face down in register on top of the wet pulp, and carefully rolled over the back of the pellon with a soft brayer until all of the drawing material was transferred. After the pellon was peeled off, the piece was again pressed, this time under full pressure, and then restraint-dried.

Pressing and drying pulp paintings

Ideally, the pulp-painted sheets should be pressed in a hydraulic press using standard pressure. This will remove most of the water and will also give the paper a smooth finish. If a more textured surface is desired, then the sheets can instead be vacuumed. Overbeaten fibres have a high rate of shrinkage and, therefore, whether you are first-pressing or vacuuming, paper made from them must be restrained while being dried. This is very important if you are planning to register a pulp painting to a printmaking matrix, since it would be very difficult to print on a cockled, distorted sheet. A forced-air drying box, constructed out of wood, with a built-in fan and a precut stack of tri-walled corrugated cardboard interleaved with blotters, can be purchased from several different suppliers. This is a great thing to invest in if you are going into production. Otherwise, you could make a simpler version like the one found in *A Papermaker's Companion* by Helen Hiebert.

PRINTING ON PULP PAINTINGS

Printing dry

Depending on the paper type and how it was dried, some sheets should be calendered before they are printed on, as this will pre-stretch and smooth out their surfaces. It would be preferable to print on dry paper whenever possible, so that rewetting won't cause any stretching or cock-

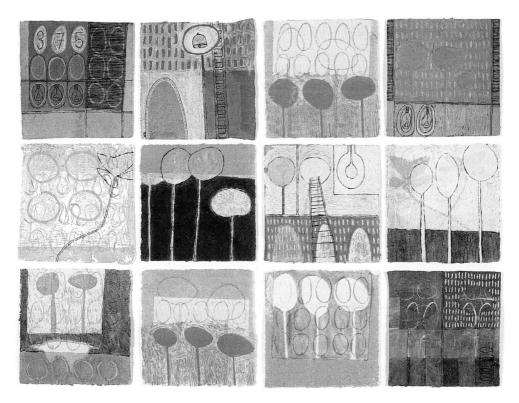

Shannon Brock, *Poor Kids Have Lawns of Dandelions*. Flax pulp painting on cotton base sheet with water-soluble pencil transfers; 12 panels, each 23 x 23 cm (9 x 9 in.); 2004. Produced by the artist. Courtesy of the artist.

ling, but this, of course, is dictated by the printmaking process being used. The screenprinted runs in Jonathan Seliger's whimsical *Fête Galante* (p.70) were printed on a smooth, dry double-layered base sheet of cotton/abaca, with stencilled pulp paint creating the background colours in the scoops, cone and logo. By digitally manipulating the image to create the information for the screenprinted runs, and by using a corresponding Mylar 'jigsaw puzzle' stencil for the pulp, Seliger ensured that the registration for both was impeccable.

Normally, lithographs are printed from a damp plate onto dry paper. When printing onto a pulp painting that was made with a substantial amount of methylcellulose, it may be necessary to fan the plate dry before printing, so that over time the water film does not reactivate the methylcellulose, which can sometimes cause hazing or scumming when certain inks are used. In the absence of water, put some dryer in each ink layer so that there will not be a problem with offset.

Dampening the paper

When dampening the paper is necessary in preparation for printing, a sheet with heavy internal sizing could require a longer soaking time for the water to make it malleable enough for embossing, collagraph and intaglio processes. Conversely, water-leaf papers, which have no sizing, become thoroughly saturated very quickly. Instead of being immersed a water-leaf paper could be misted on both sides with a fine-spray bottle. When dampening paper that has been pulp-painted, it is a good idea not to oversaturate the sheets, because, when it is being peeled from certain types of textural plates after printing, the overbeaten pulp used as the paint could separate from the base sheet if that sheet was not made with similarly overbeaten pulp. April Gornik's *Halang Bay* (opposite) combines two intaglio plates with overbeaten linen-pulp paint on cotton base sheets. Instead of soaking the sheets in a tray of water, as is commonly done in preparation for printing an intaglio plate, they were dampened on each side with a sponge, and then left in plastic overnight.

Accepting the ink layer

Oil-based ink will trap differently according to the paper used. It will appear matt where it falls into the less-beaten fibre of the backer sheet, and can appear shiny where it sits on the overbeaten pulp paint, which is less

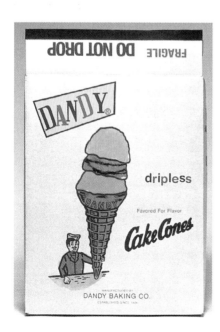

Jonathan Seliger, *Fête Galante*. Stencilled pulp painting and silkscreen on cotton/ abaca and pigmented cotton, 51 x 33.5 cm (20¼ x 13¼ x 6½ in.), 2004. Produced at Dieu Donné Papermill, collaborating master papermaker: Megan Moorehouse. Collaborating master printer: Courtney Healy at Lower Eastside Printshop. Courtesy of Dieu Donné Papermill.

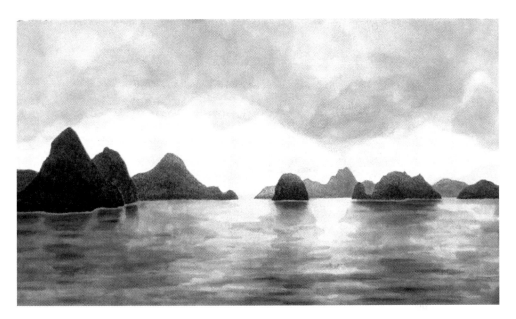

April Gornik, *Halang Bay*. Cotton base sheet with linen pulp paint and etching, 44.5 x 73.5 cm (17$^1/_2$ x 29 in.), 2004. Published by Dieu Donné Papermill. Collaborating Master Papermaker: Megan Moorehouse. Collaborating Master Printer: Julio D'Amario. Courtesy of Dieu Donné Papermill.

absorbent. This condition is most obvious in lithographic-, monotype- and relief-printed flats. Fibres 'picking' from the handmade sheet can also be a problem (see 'Sizing' above) when using tacky ink on undersized paper, so tack modification may be necessary.

Drying the finished print

Sheets printed damp should be restraint-dried as always, so that no cockling or distortion will occur.

5 · WATERMARKS

by Eileen Foti

Watermarking is a subtle yet striking way to make an image. A watermark is a translucent design in a sheet of paper, best viewed when held up to the light or when couched on top of a dark-coloured base sheet. The first Western-style watermarks were produced in Italy in 1282. They were made by sewing thin wire patterns to the mesh surface of the mould, so that when a sheet was formed the wet pulp would be thinner in the areas where it covered the wire and thicker where it accumulated on the mesh. When the sheet was pressed and dried, the watermarked design would become visible as light passed through.

Historically, watermarked designs or emblems were a way of identifying the work of a specific paper mill or artisan. By the early 1800s, when paper was being manufactured by machine in continuous rolls, the dandy roll had been invented as a way of introducing images like watermarks into the paper's wet surface. Dandy-roll cylinders are first covered in either wove or laid textured mesh and then decorated with a raised metal design, so that both textures transfer into the damp pulp on contact. In the mid-1800s in England, 'light and shade' watermarks were invented. Also known as chiaroscuro watermarks, they allowed for the creation of tonal ranges in the paper's surface when held up to the light. In addition to creating beautiful, artistic images, being extremely difficult to reproduce they eventually became a means of safeguarding against the counterfeiting of currency.

When you consider that the process of making watermarks is over 750 years old, it is exciting to think that artists working in paper today are still finding innovative ways of creating them. This chapter will explore some of their techniques, both historic and contemporary.

FIBRE PREPARATION

Papermakers can choose from several different fibres, including cotton, hemp, flax, linen, or abaca, and sometimes two or more of these in combination with each other. They need to consider the characteristic of each fibre, in terms of opacity, transparency and colour, as well as how they will perform with the intended type of watermark that is being produced. The pulp should be free of decorative inclusions such as threads or flower petals, as they will obstruct the watermark's clarity.

Beating

In order to yield the crispest image possible, the pulps used for making Western-style watermarks are usually mechanically beaten until they are quite short in length. Conversely, Eastern-style fibre being used for the Japanese methods described below can be prepared in the traditional manner and beaten by hand, which will keep the fibres long.

Additives

Some papermakers choose to add fillers to their pulp to make the finished sheets smoother and more opaque. In certain cases, this can help exaggerate the contrast between the lighter (thinner layer of pulp) and darker (thicker layer of pulp) areas on the finished watermarked sheets. These fillers include calcium carbonate, kaolin (also referred to as china clay) and titanium dioxide pigment. A printmaker should note that these fillers make the paper's surface smoother, harder and sometimes less absorbent. Ink will tend to sit on the surface and not drop in as far as it would if the paper did not contain one of these fillers. Whether or not this is desirable depends upon which printmaking process will be used.

Pigments

Commonly, watermarked sheets are made from pulp that is either natural in colour or slightly tinted. Whether or not to use pigmented pulps is sometimes determined by how watermarks will be used: for instance, couching a light-coloured watermarked sheet onto a heavily pigmented base sheet, or couching a pigmented watermarked sheet onto a white base sheet – both can be striking. A pigmented watermarked sheet made from a translucent fibre like abaca will have a stained-glass quality when held up to the light, while another made from pulp that is more opaque will yield an end result that can be much more subtle.

Sizing

If the finished watermarked sheets are to be printed upon, then it is preferable to add internal sizing. (Please refer to the Sizing section in the Pulp Painting chapter.)

TYPES OF WATERMARKS

There are many different methods for creating a watermark and attaching it to a mould. For example, wire can produce imagery that is linear or calligraphic; chiaroscuro watermarks can appear tonal or photographic; self-adhering films like vinyl or contact paper can be cut into a multitude of shapes; and fabric paint can make fluid, whimsical lines. Below are selected examples of these and other methods. Keep in mind, as with printmaking, that the watermark should be attached to the screen in reverse orientation, so that the finished sheet of paper will read correctly.

Wire

Thinking in Water (opposite, top) by William Kentridge is a suite of three images in pigmented cotton linter and linen-rag pulp. Two of the panels contain wire watermarks that were made from bending and soldering 16- and 18-gauge round copper wire stock. Once completed, they were sewn onto the surfaces of two laid moulds (opposite, below). After the watermarked sheets were couched, Kentridge pulp-painted text across them with squeeze bottles containing the same pulp stock mixed with formation aid. The end results are suites of subtle if not anonymous sheets that only reveal their messages when held up to the light.

'Light and shade' (chiaroscuro) watermarks

The lengthy process begins with the image being carved into wax as a shallow relief. The finished wax relief is coated with powdered graphite, electroplated, and, from this, male and female dies are produced. Next, a piece of wire cloth is annealed and pressed between the two plates so that it will take on their forms. Once completed, this mesh is sewn onto a regular papermaking mould. When a sheet is formed, the thickest concentrations of pulp, which collect in the lowest parts of the relief, will appear the darkest in the finished paper; and the thinnest concentrations, which collect on the highest parts of the mould, will appear as the lightest areas in the finished sheet.

Canadian papermaker Brian Queen puts a contemporary spin on this age-old technique by using digital resources to create an aluminum die directly from a photograph or drawing, eliminating the need for the laborious process of sculpting a wax relief and then plating it. To make his untitled portrait watermark of Dard Hunter (page 76), Queen scanned and

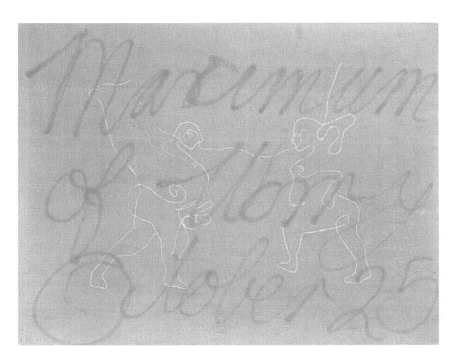

ABOVE William Kentridge, *Thinking in Water* (detail), 2002. Wire watermark and pulp painting on cotton/linen base sheet. Suite of three each 45.5 x 61 cm (18 x 24 in.). Published by Dieu Donné Papermill. Collaborating master papermakers: Mina Takahashi and Megan Moorehouse. Metalsmith: Michael Fitzgerald. Courtesy of Dieu Donné Papermill.

BELOW Wire watermark attached to papermaking mould. Courtesy of Dieu Donné Papermill.

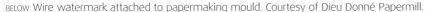

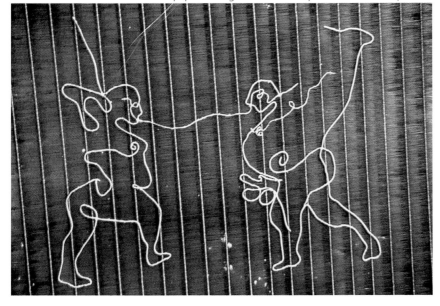

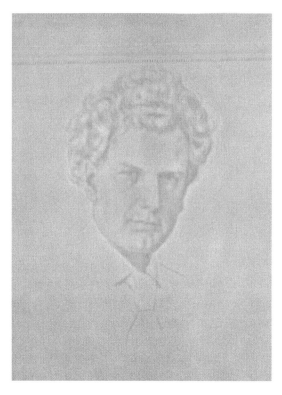

Brian Queen, *Untitled portrait watermark of Dard Hunter,* Chiaroscuro watermarked cotton sheet, 25 x 20 cm (10 x 8 in.), 2001. Published by *Hand Papermaking Magazine* for its portfolio, *Watermarks in Handmade Paper: Modern and Historic*. Produced by the artist. Courtesy of the artist.

manipulated the originally drawn image. Then the computer guided a three-dimensional milling or engraving machine to incise the image into a piece of aluminum. From this engraving, he devised a way to emboss the annealed bronze mesh material with his press. Queen pulled sheets with very short second-cut cotton pulp, and the results are breathtaking.

Adhesive materials

Creating watermarks by attaching any among a wide variety of self-adhering materials to a mould can yield wonderful results. These materials include magnetic stripping, tape, contact paper, vinyl press type and many others. Not only are these materials readily accessible and easy to cut, they can also be easily attached, removed and reattached to a dry mould. They can also be stuck down to an extra piece of screen material placed on the mould's surface during production, and later removed so that the mould can be used for another project and the watermark remains intact for future use.

In Amanda Guest's *Deep Blue Page V* (see p. 67), thin strips of strapping tape were adhered to the surface of a mould to create rows of crisp linear watermarks (see the Pulp Painting and Stencilling Techniques section in the Pulp Painting chapter for a more complete description).

The text watermark in Mel Bochner's piece *Language Is Not Transparent* (opposite, top) was made from layered self-adhering signage vinyl that was typeset and cut by computer. The white abaca watermarked sheets were couched onto black cotton base sheets, making the tones created by the layered watermark more apparent.

Mel Bochner, *Language is not transparent*. Watermarked translucent abaca on black cotton base sheet, 101.5 x 76 cm (40 x 30 in.); 1999. Published by Dieu Donné Papermill. Collaborating master papermakers: Mina Takahashi and Pat Almonrode. Courtesy of Dieu Donné Papermill.

BELOW White watermarked sheet being couched onto the black cotton base sheet. Courtesy of Dieu Donné Papermill.

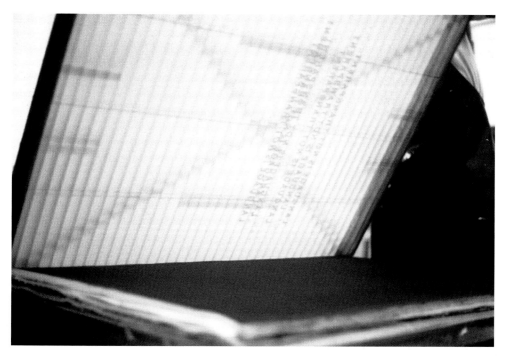

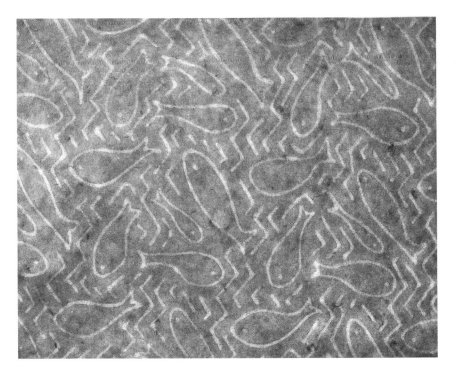

Wendy Cain, *Untitled (Fish Watermark)*. Fabric paint watermark, 20 x 25 cm (8 x 10 in.), 2001. Published by *Hand Papermaking Magazine* for its portfolio, *Watermarks in Handmade paper: Modern and Historic*. Produced by the artist. Courtesy of the artist.

Fabric paint

A quick way to draw fluid watermarks is to use small-tipped squeeze bottles of fabric paint (also referred to as 'puffy paint') on No-See-Um netting or woven screen material. When a sheet is pulled, the screening with the raised beads of paint on top sits on the surface of a regular mould. Wendy Cain adapted this method to create her luminous untitled piece, made from richly pigmented abaca (above).

Photosilkscreen watermarks

Just as watermarks are a means of identifying papermakers, fingerprints are a way to identify us all. Gangolf Ulbricht explores this theme in *Thumbprint* (opposite, top), for which he scanned his own thumbprint and manipulated it in order to produce a positive film. He built up a thick layer of photo-emulsion by applying several coats of it to a silkscreen stretched on an aluminum frame. He exposed the film onto the screen and then washed off the excess emulsion. He used that silkscreen as the paper-making mould, with the remaining emulsion thumbprint as the water-marking device. Ulbricht combines cotton linters, flax, hemp and high-grade wood cellulose with starch, china clay and calcium carbonate to make his extremely fine pulp.

Watermarks inspired by Japanese lace paper

The Japanese technique of *Rakusui-shi* (or 'falling-water paper') has been used for hundreds of years. Contemporary artists like Kristin Kavanagh have adapted its basics to create new and innovative work. Kavanagh's untitled piece (right) is made from two layers of *gampi*, which she prepared and beat in the traditional way. Each base sheet was formed on a Western-style mould that she first covered with

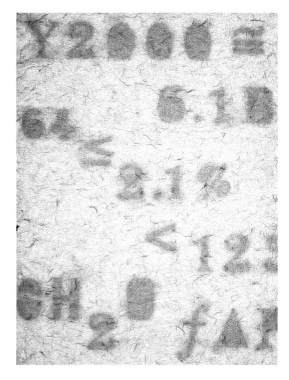

ABOVE RIGHT Gangolf Ulbricht, *Thumbprint*. Watermark made from photosilkscreen mesh, 25 x 20 cm (10 x 8 in.), 2001. Published by *Hand Papermaking Magazine* for its portfolio, *Watermarks in Handmade paper: Modern and Historic*. Produced by the artist. Courtesy of the artist.

RIGHT Kristin Kavanagh, *Untitled (Web)*. Watermarked *gampi* sheet with pig-mented *gampi*, 25 x 20 cm (10 x 8 in.), 2001. Published by *Hand Papermaking* magazine for its portfolio, *Watermarks in Handmade Paper: Modern and Historic*. Produced by the artist. Courtesy of the artist.

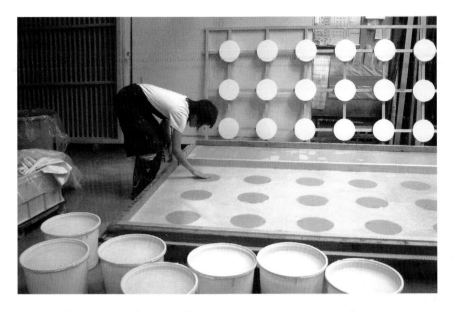

Watermarking on a grand scale at the Awagami Factory, Fuji Papermills, Japan, 2005.

No-See-Um netting. She pulled a very thin sheet of *gampi* and, before couching it, placed a Mylar spider-web stencil on top and sprayed water onto it to break up the exposed paper's surface, creating a series of tiny random dots in the open areas. When the Mylar was lifted off, the web pattern underneath was intact, creating a strong contrast with its now 'lacy', ethereal background. Kavanagh couched that sheet. The next layer was also made with tinted *gampi* and stencils, and once formed it was couched onto the spider-web layer. After being pressed, the sheets were dried on wooden boards.

PRINTING ON WATERMARKED PAPERS

Many of the same considerations that exist for printing on handmade paper in general apply when printing on watermarked sheets, in terms of dampening and redrying, and how certain inks will trap on sheets made from less beaten or overbeaten pulp. (See the section on Printing on Pulp Paintings in the Pulp Painting chapter.)

Interesting results can be gained from experimenting with printing over, as well as printing on, the backs of watermarked sheets. The transparency or translucency of the ink films can also be explored.

6 · PAPERMAKING FROM NATIVE SCOTTISH PLANTS

by Charmian Pollok

As a printmaker, you will probably think about paper more than the majority of people for whom paper is so ubiquitous as to be taken for granted. It is, in fact, a very special and ancient material occupying an important place in our society. You will be aware, as you make your prints, of how the paper you select can affect them. There is a huge range of papers for printmaking available to buy, but another option is to make your own papers.

Making paper from plants is a magical thing to do, and can be a source of wonderful and unique papers for the printmaker, as each plant produces its own distinct paper. The gentle, natural colours can provide a subtle background to complement your print. I have successfully used my own handmade papers for etchings, relief prints, monoprints, collagraphs and digital prints. These papers form an integral part of my working methods and artworks. There is no reason why you could not also try using your own papers for other printmaking methods. But be warned – it can become an obsession! I first became interested in papermaking while studying for my printmaking degree at Glasgow School of Art, and it is something I have pursued with increasing intensity ever since. Making your own unique papers adds an extra dimension to your art works, and materials are readily obtainable in the countryside, in gardens and shops. Making your own papers also gives you control over every element of the process.

One of the first and most important things to bear in mind is to record everything, including plant names (both common and botanical), the places where they were gathered, the time of year, the weather, the part of the plant that was used and each step of the process as you make the paper. You should then be able to replicate any particular paper, although it will never be an exact match. Try to make as much paper in one session as you think you will need, plus some extra, particularly if you are planning to print off an edition; and buy yourself a good botanical guide.

RECORDING THE PAPERMAKING PROCESS

Keeping a careful and detailed record will provide you with a valuable data resource that will enable you to make further, similar sheets. While it is obviously not essential to understand Latin, it is very useful at least to be familiar with the botanical Latin names of the plants you are using, not least because these names are understood by botanists all over the world. This knowledge would be an aid not just in identifying plants as you travel but also in helping you to identify which plants might be useful for paper-making, as plants which are from the same botanical families may share characteristics which would lend them to the hand-papermaking process. For example, the wild yellow iris, popularly known as yellow flag, is, in Latin, *Iris pseudacorus*, plant family *Iridaceae*. The popular garden plant and sometime garden escapee *crocosmia* (sometimes referred to as *montbretia*) is also from the family *Iridaceae*. These two plants can be processed in the same way.

The following is the type of information you should record. The record should comprise three sections: fibre gathering, fibre preparation and sheet formation.

1. Fibre gathering

This section should include the following information on the plant: its botanical name, common name and plant-family name; the location where it was harvested, the weather at the time it was harvested, the method of harvesting, and the date and season when it was harvested; the part of the plant that was used; the dry weight of the harvested fibre (this will enable you to calculate how much alkali you need to cook the fibre); and any additional comments.

2. Fibre preparation

Precooking preparation

Depending on the plant part used, record here whether you simply cut the fibres into short lengths, as with a grass fibre such as rush, or a leaf fibre such as iris; whether a tough leaf fibre needs to be decorticated (outer skin scraped), e.g. pineapple; or whether the fibre needs to be retted (in water or alkali or field-retted) before being cut or chopped prior to soaking. Did you use scissors or a garden shredder to cut up the plant? Did the plant part need to be beaten with a mallet before processing as might be sary with thick nettle or thistle stems? Did you strip off leaves before chopping up stems; did you steam or scrape the plant to remove the outer bark? And so on. To enable them to take up the alkali efficiently, fibres benefit from being soaked either in water or, if tough, in water plus alkali before being cooked in the alkali of your choice. Note the soaking time.

Cooking
Record here the alkali used (e.g., sodium carbonate); the quantity used (usually 20% of the dry weight of your fibre if you are using sodium carbonate); the volume of water; and the cooking time.

Rinsing
Here you should record the time and method, e.g., cooked fibre tied up in a muslin bag and then rinsed under the tap for 25 minutes. Test regularly for pH.

Beating
First record the equipment used (e.g., kitchen blender, Hollander beater, mallet); then note the beating time: did you, for instance, beat all the fibres the same way and for the same length of time, or did you beat most of the pulp in the blender and then add to this in the vat some hand-beaten pulp to give a variation in fibre length?

Additives
Did you add any other substances, such as size, pigments, dyes or buffering agent?

Additional comments
Anything else worth noting.

3. Sheet formation
Additives
Record any additives you put into the vat, such as size or formation aid. Also note the quantity added.

Method
Did you form your sheet by Japanese or Western techniques? Did you use pouring, or perhaps a deckle box?

Couching method

Did you use felts, kitchen cloths or another material on which to lay your sheet, or did you lay it onto Perspex or glass?

Pressing

Did you use a book press or a hydraulic press, or did you sponge-press your paper?

Drying

Was the paper restraint-dried, or did you leave it to dry on the mould, or perhaps on Perspex? Did you iron-dry it or did you hang up the wet sheets on their felts to dry? How long did it take to dry?

Finishing

Did you size the sheets? If so, which size did you use?

Colour

You will find that this will vary according to the season in which the plant was harvested.

Type

Is your paper soft, crisp, etc.? Did it shrink as it dried? How absorbent is it?

Size and yield

How big are your sheets? How many sheets did the amount of pulp make?

Additional comments

Anything else worth noting.

Experimentation is the key to discovery. You can try to make paper from just about any plant, although some will be easier to work with than others, while some will yield better, stronger paper. There are many variables, such as the weather and the season, which affect this process. Take one plant, try making paper from it at different times of the year, and you will end up with different papers each time.

You must also bear in mind the requirements of the particular print-making method you are going to use, as you can make your paper to suit the requirements of each printmaking process. You can use your hand-made papers on their own or in combination with commercially made papers, such as in the chine collé technique (see the Printing on Handmade

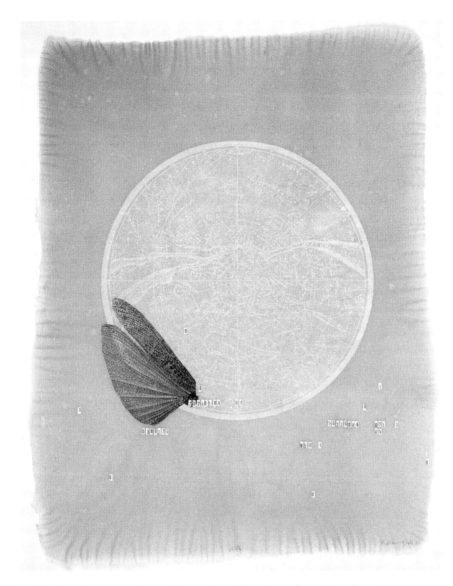

Eileen Foti; *Air*, 2001; 28 x 21.5 cm (11 x 8½ in); handmade paper, inclusions, lithography.

Papers chapter). You can make your paper purely from one plant or you can use a basis of cotton linters or one of the other part-prepared pulps that are commercially available (see the section below on sources of pulp for the hand-papermaker). Recycled offcuts from commercially made printing papers make a good-quality base to which you can add some of your own native-plant pulps. You might consider this if you are going to print a deeply bitten etching plate, which would require a heavier and softer-quality paper than would be necessary for a wood engraving. Always consider which qualities are needed for the particular printmaking technique you are going to use. The hand-papermaking process can then be tailored to the type of printmaking method you have chosen. For example, if you are going to hand-burnish then you will need a more lightweight paper than might be needed if you were using a press. I have used fine, pure native-plant papers for monochrome etchings, but not with deeply bitten plates and not for prints with many different colours, which would need to go through the press several times. I have also used my own papers for digital prints.

You will use different plant parts depending on the plants selected and gathered. In some plants it may be the seed head, as in the cotton plant; in others it may be the leaves, as in the iris plant. In yet other plants it may be the inner bark, e.g., silver birch. The following recipe is suitable for plants from which the stem, as in grasses, or the leaves are used. These are the easiest for you to process. Some of the plants in this category are:

Sources of pulp

The **soft rush** (*Juncus effusis*), of the family *Juncaceae*, is a native, clump-forming perennial growing in boggy and wet ground, measuring from 30 to 150 cm high. Cut the stems but do not take up the roots. The plant will grow back. Depending on when the plant is harvested – either spring or autumn – the paper will be green or brownish. It makes a lovely crisp paper that is fairly easy to process and prints beautifully. This is one of my favourite pulps.

The **common reed** (*Phragmites australis*), of the family *Gramineae*, is a native perennial common in marshes and shallow water growing in large beds. It has tough stems but when chopped up makes a strong blond-beige paper. The flower heads can be included for further decorative effect. It measures from 150 to 300 cm high.

Reed grass (*Phalaris arundinacea*), again a member of the *Gramineae* family, is a native perennial commonly found throughout the British Isles in damp places by rivers, lakes, marshes and meadows. Reed grass is easy to process, although the paper it makes is not quite as strong as that of the common reed.

Iris pseudacorus, of the family *Iridaceae*, is the 'yellow flag' iris. Use the fleshy leaves of this perennial, which grows by marshes, boggy ground and fresh water. You can cut the leaves of this plant to process them straight

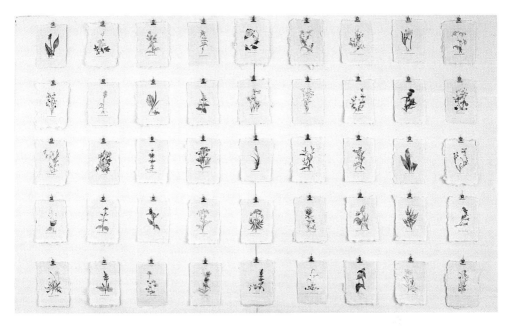

Charmian Pollok, NN40/50: *Epitome of Summer,* overall size 200 x 244 cm (78¾ x 96 in.). 45 embossed digital prints on handmade *kozo* paper, each measuring 17 x 12 cm (6¾ x 4¾ in.), 2003.

away. If you harvest in springtime, cut only the outer leaves and cut from near the base of the plant, which will allow it to grow on from the centre.

Crocosmia x crocosmiiflora, of the family *Iridaceae* and also sometimes known as *montbretia*, is a common garden plant which has also naturalised in many parts of the country. Like the iris it can be harvested in spring or autumn. I grow this plant in my garden, where I leave it to die back naturally in the autumn and over the winter, when nature does part of the preparation for me in a process known as 'retting'. As the plant is exposed to the weather, much of the fleshy, non-cellulose, unwanted part of the plant will break down, and you will quite clearly see the cellulose fibres appearing. In this state you can safely add some finely chopped, overwintered fibres to a base pulp to give added interest, or you can cook it 'neat' in a mild alkali in greater quantities to make a good, strong, pure crocosmia paper. It sometimes pays not to be a tidy gardener! The paper made from this overwintered fibre will yield a strong, brownish paper, as opposed to what you will get from the same plant earlier in the year when the leaves are green. If it is mixed with a cotton base, the colour will be lightened.

You can store this or the other plants mentioned in their dried states for later use. You can also store your finished plant pulps by drying or freezing them. In both cases they will need to be rehydrated briefly before they are used. A quick whizz in the blender will do.

Other plants to try which are easy to use are:

Daffodil: the leaves and stems. You can add small pieces of the petals to the prepared pulp – although you may notice the petals changing colour over time – or you can dry and press the petals to be ready for later use.

Celery: simply chop up and use as per the method below.

Leeks: chop off the root part, composting it if you can, and then chop up the remaining parts, green and white – the ratio here will determine the colour – and follow the method.

Nettles: can be used fresh or dried. If fresh, wearing gloves, strip off the leaves and lightly scrape the stems to remove the outer layer. You can omit this stage if the stems are very slender, as it is a rather fiddly process. If the stems are stout, bash them with a mallet or rolling pin before chopping them into small pieces and cooking them with the alkali. This will help them to take up the alkali better when cooking.

Method

1. Always use a large stainless-steel pan with a good lid, and protect your hands by wearing gloves, especially when using the alkali needed to break down the fibres. Fill the pan with about eight litres of water and start heating it before adding the plant, processed as below. There should always be enough space in the pan for the plant to be able to move around during cooking.

2. Cut up the plants into small pieces. This is particularly important if you are going to use a blender to beat the pulp. The pieces may need to be as small as 1 cm ($\frac{1}{2}$ in.). You can cut them further, if necessary, when they are cooked. If the fibres are too long they will tangle around the blades of the liquidiser. It might be tedious cutting them so small, but it saves frustration in the long run! If you have access to a garden shredder, you can use that. Next, if the plants are dry, put the cut-up pieces in water to soak before cooking. This is not necessary if the plants are fresh, and therefore moist. The soaking causes the cell walls to swell, allowing the plant to take up the alkali more easily and efficiently during cooking.

   Some very tough plants benefit from a soak in an alkaline solution, rather than plain water, before cooking. When this is done rinse off, then make up a fresh alkaline solution for the actual cooking process.

3. For every 500 g (1 lb) of dried fibres you will need 100 g (3½ oz) of alkali to break them down. With experience you will learn that you can adjust the quantity of alkali, as some plants may need less. Certain tough plants will need to be cooked again if they have not broken down after 2–3 hours. Make up fresh alkali for the second cooking.

   My preferred alkali is soda ash, or sodium carbonate (Na_2CO_3), which is available from some printmaking or papermaking suppliers (see List of Suppliers). Add this to the pan of still heating, but not yet boiling, water. It will dissolve easily. It is possible to substitute washing soda, a more easily available alkali, but this is less pure than soda ash because it contains various other chemicals. These will vary from brand to brand, but may leave a residue in the paper. However, do not worry too much if, for reasons of availability, this is the alkali you have to use. Finally, if the plant is really tough you may need to use caustic soda to break it down. (See below for my warning over the use of caustic soda.)

4. Fibres like soft rush are hollow and thus inclined to float to the top of the container in which they are soaking, so weight them down. You could try bashing them a little bit with a wooden mallet before soaking them. Do this if you have any plant with tough stems to process – nettle or thistle, for example.

5. If you are using fresh plant fibres, you will need to measure out your alkali by measuring the water in the pan in which you are cooking your plant rather than by weighing the fibre. The ratio of alkali to water is about 15 g (½ oz) per litre (or quart) of water, the alkali being added as the water is heating.

   A word of warning if you are using caustic soda: it is VERY important that you add the caustic soda to a small amount of cold water first – that is, before pouring this solution into the pan of unheated cooking water – otherwise it can fizz up alarmingly.

6. Put a lid on the pot – this reduces the smell if you are cooking the material indoors – but keep stirring the plant fibres from time to time.

7. Though you can make paper from a very small amount of plant material (which is fine for a sample), to make a reasonable number of sheets try and gather a good amount of plant stuff. It is difficult to give a precise amount, but you'll learn from experience how much you will need. It reduces greatly in the cooking – think of cooking spinach! Weigh it before processing.

8. To test whether the fibre is cooked sufficiently, test it periodically, perhaps every 45 minutes or so. A plant such as daffodil will cook much more quickly than soft rush or common reed. Remove a sample of fibre from the pan; if you can squidge it in your fingers and easily pull it apart, it will be done.

9. The fibre will need to be rinsed thoroughly to bring it back to a neutral pH. Line a sieve or colander with fine-mesh muslin and tip the plant material into it. Do this carefully in a sink. I often use a colander in preference to a sieve, as a sieve needs to be held, whereas a colander has a base on which it can stand, thus freeing you to use both hands. You must rinse the fibre in cold water until the water runs completely clear and reads at neutral on the pH-indicator strips. It is sometimes recommended that, in fact, you leave it just on the alkaline side of neutral in order to allow for the inevitable shift towards acid which happens to paper over the course of time. This way you should end up with the pH at neutral. All of this rinsing could well take 20 minutes or more.

10. It is often said that paper is made in the beating. If you have access to a Hollander beater then so much the better, but most likely you will have the options of either hand-beating, or using a kitchen blender, or a combination of the two methods. Combining the two methods is often a good way of preparing your pulp, giving you a mixture of long and short fibres. The kitchen blender chops rather than fibrillates the fibres but is, nonetheless, the mechanical gadget you are most likely to have access to. It will provide a good base pulp to which you can add some longer, hand-beaten fibres, which will add to the strength of the paper as well as adding visual and textural interest.

Consider whether a paper will need to be sized. This can be done during or after the papermaking process. If the paper needs to be moistened prior to printing, then consider how this will affect it. You can either moisten by misting the paper with water from a plant-mister or you can layer your papers between moistened blotters. Be aware of the possibility of too much moisture causing cockling as the print dries; for this reason, it may have to be dried under pressure. Ensure also that the paper is evenly dampened before it is used, and blot to remove excess moisture.

The paper can be dried in various ways prior to printing. It can be left to dry on the mould, which will give a more textured surface, or the damp sheet of paper can be turned out onto a sheet of glass or Perspex, which

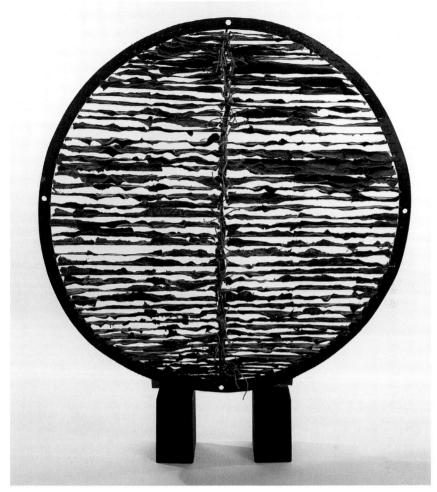

Charmian Pollok, *Boundary: Creag A'Mhadaidh*. 100 x 120 cm (39½ x 47¼ in.); iron, paper handmade from recycled workwear, Scottish oak and jute, 2001.

will give a smooth, glassy surface. Again, your chosen printmaking method will determine the drying method you choose.

It is possible to smooth the paper after is has dried by calendering it. This can be easily achieved by laying the sheet of paper on the clean back of a printing plate, covering it with tissue and running it through the etching press; or by laying it against a smooth surface of some sort, such as pristine mount board with a piece of board both top and bottom to form a sandwich, and then placing it in a book press for half an hour. You can also smooth it by hand-burnishing it, though this can be a bit laborious if the sheet of paper is of any great size.

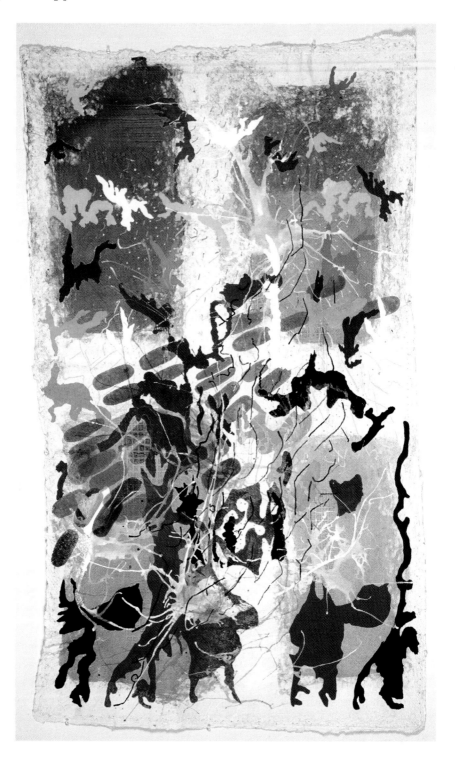

7 · PRINTING ON HANDMADE PAPERS

Experimentation is the name of the game when preparing your own handmade paper to print on: after preparing your pulp, make a few sheets – vary them in sizing, surface texture, colour, thickness, etc. – which you can then use for proofing your prints. When printing on your own hand-made papers, it is important to take the following points into consideration:

1. The way in which the ink is going to be absorbed by the paper in question is crucial to achieving a crisp and clear impression, especially since the introduction of water-based inks to almost all print disciplines. The preva-lence of so-called safe printmaking, whereby water-based inks, paints and, in some cases, gouache and combinations of paints and binders are used, means the sizing of the sheet must be taken into consideration.

2. The length of paper fibre used, how that fibre was beaten, and the fibre softness and absorbency should also be taken into account. The print performance will also be determined by whether you use a Western-style mould and deckle or a Japanese *sugeta* to form the sheets.

3. The smoothness of the finished sheet, whether it needs to be calendered or printed damp for maximum effect, along with how pliant the sheet is, should also be taken into account.

PAPERS SUITABLE FOR OFFSET AND STONE LITHOGRAPHY PRINTING

The main difference between offset-lithography printing and direct-lithog-raphy printing is that in the former the inked image is transferred from plate to offset blanket to paper, and in the latter method the paper is placed directly onto the surface of the stone. The pressure applied when printing

OPPOSITE Anne Q. McKeown, *Parade's ending*, 165 x 96.5 cm (65 x 38 in.). Cotton, bleached abaca, pigmented overbeaten hemp, acrylic paint, 2003.

a direct image is less than the pressure exerted by the offset press, and this difference in pressure can be a determining factor in the type of paper you can use. When using your own handmade papers, it is always advisable to test a small amount first, bearing in mind the sizing of the sheet. This is especially relevant when using several colour overlays.

When working with handmade papers, I have found that, in general, an evenly sized, absorbent paper that is acid-free and resistant to picking will best accept ink, detail and tonal quality in printing from an offset press. Interestingly, some unsized papers will also print well. These seem to perform best in printing directly from a slightly dampened stone, as offset can produce picking, especially when the paper contains long fibres.

Picking, whereby the paper fibres can be pulled from the sheet by the tack of the ink whilst printing, can be a problem. From personal experience, I have found that it occurs more frequently when one is printing from an offset press, as opposed to printing from a direct litho press. Qualities such as the softness and texture of the paper should also be considered. Textured paper may be calendered before use with lithography, to create a smooth surface, which is desirable if you want to maintain detail. To calender your sheet, run it through the direct press (you can also use an etching press) twice in the same direction under a good, even printing pressure. The press pressure, too, plays an important role in printing, especially when it comes to offset.

ADDITIVES

Chemical additives play a very important role in the production of paper, and can impart many properties to the sheet. Colouring, coating or strengthening the sheet, or rendering it water-absorbent or water-resistant, are just a few examples of additive treatments that determine the type of paper. For the printmaker wishing to make his or her own paper, however, sizing will probably be the primary consideration.

SIZING

The performance of a paper is greatly determined by the method by which it is sized, and the type of size used. As far as printing is concerned, a sized sheet renders a much crisper image, one that is both bleed-resistant and water-repellent, and is also resistant to picking. This applies when

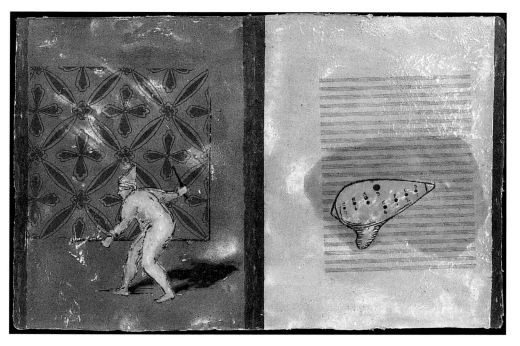

Georgia Deal; *Family Secret*; 61 x 102 cm (24 x 40 in.); handmade paper with silkscreen print.

used with either water-based or oil-based media. However, it is worth noting that size in the paper can soften up after several colour overlays, thus affecting the printed image. (See the sections on sizing in the Setting Up chapter and in Eileen Foti's Pulp Painting chapter for further explanation on sizing.)

Recipe for external gelatin sizing

Dissolve 1 oz (30 g) of gelatin in a litre of hot water, adding the powder to the liquid, not the other way round.

Paper can be coated in two different ways:

1. Dip a wide, soft-haired brush into a container of hot water and then into the gelatin solution. Brush across the sheet in one direction only, using smooth strokes, then repeat on the reverse side of the sheet.

2. Immerse the sheet of paper into a deep tray containing the solution, then immediately remove it and hang it up to dry.

COLOUR

'Colour' in a printed or drawn image can refer to either the ink employed in the making of that image or the paper used for the substrate. Coloured paper dates to before the 18th century and was made from dyed rags – white, brown and blue being the most common. Nowadays, paper may be coloured in many different ways, but, whatever the method employed, lightfastness should be a primary consideration, as dyes, being active chemicals, have a tendency to fade in sunlight.

AQUEOUS DISPERSED PIGMENTS

Favoured by some papermakers, these are safer to use and more archival than dye, and also easy to mix together, like paint. They do not have to be ground before use, unlike artists' powdered pigments, which nevertheless can also be used in the coloration of pulp. The pigmentation of pulp takes place after it has been beaten. For very even coloration, pigment may be added gradually to the wet pulp in the Hollander for a few minutes just before the end of the beating cycle. Check the colour of the pulp water as you do it: if colour is still bleeding from the pulp, add a few drops of retention aid (or refer to the product instructions for using these pigments*). The retention aid literally *retains* the pigment, attaching it to the pulp so that colour will not bleed out. Retention aid is generally added to the pulp after it is beaten.

DYE

Dyes are either organic or synthetic water-soluble substances, and are divided into different types: soluble dyes, acid dyes, direct dyes, plant dyes, fibre-reactive dyes, etc. Direct dyes are strongly attracted to cellulose, attaching themselves to the cellulose molecules to form a firm bond, whereas acid dyes, with no affinity for cellulose, require either rosin or alum as a fixer. Dyes such as Dylon can be bought from fabric shops, art stores and supermarkets, and work well with cotton linters. Concentrated dye solutions can also be obtained from paper mills. Fibre-reactive dyes

---

* These are available from Carriage House Paper and Lee Scott McDonald – see List of Suppliers. Aqueous dispersed pigments for colouring pulp are also available from papermaking suppliers.

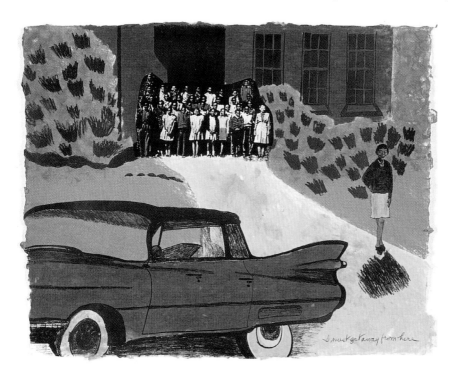

Joan Eta Byrd, *I must get away from here*, 1998. Lithograph, handmade paper, pulp painting chine collé, 40 x 50 cm (16 x 20 in.).

will often produce strong colours, and are mixed with soda ash and salt for permanence.

Finally, be aware that pulps dyed different colours are not so easy to blend together, as each dyed fibre tends to retain its original colour. (See the chapter on Pulp Painting by Eileen Foti for information on how to colour pulp.)

DYEING WITH PLANTS AND NATURAL MATERIALS

Early papers were coloured with a range of natural ingredients – e.g., berries, indigo, a natural dye like cochineal, and logwood – which were readily available in Europe and used in the dyeing of cloth. Exotic-sounding sources for colouring pulp included lapis lazuli, woad and verdigris. Retaining the base fibres of plants such as onion and monbretia in their natural state will also produce interesting, natural-coloured sheets of paper. (See also Charmian Pollok's chapter on Papermaking with Native Scottish Plants.)

POWDERED PIGMENTS

These pigments can be added to water and ground to a paste in a pestle and mortar. Some may require the addition of gum arabic or alum to enable the fibres to retain the pigment, as some pigments contain different properties, e.g., inorganic coloured pigments and synthetic organic pigments (see supplier's instructions). Artists' powdered pigments can be purchased from artists' suppliers such as Cornelissen's in London.

RAGS

Colour will of course be determined by the colour of rag one is beating; items such as denim jeans will produce interesting paper. For an in-depth guide to colouring paper, refer to Elaine Koretsky's *Color for the Hand Papermaker*, and also Helen Hiebert's *The Papermaker's Companion* (see Bibliography).

CHINE COLLÉ

Chine collé, or *papier collé* as it is sometimes known, is a process whereby a thin sheet of paper is printed and adhered simultaneously to a larger and heavier hand- or mould-made paper sheet. The French word *collé* literally means 'stuck down', and *Chine* refers to China – a reference perhaps to the invention of paper. Usually, this paper is a thin Japanese paper, such as *gampi* or *yumato*. Handmade papers work well, as long as they are very thin. It is probably a good idea to size these papers, as picking could occur from an unsized sheet. Experiment with local plant papers, as these can give interesting results.

Historically, European artists during the late 19th and early 20th centuries, such as Odilon Redon, used the process extensively for lithography. It works best when printing from a direct press. It is also feasible to apply the *collé* sections first to the backing sheet of paper by placing them carefully in register and running them through an etching press. The glues used in this process must be archival and acid-free.

Modern approaches to *collé* printing involve using pressure-sensitive polymer adhesives. Rhoplex N-580, made by Rohm and Haas in the USA, and Primal E-1961 both have a high pH value and thus render good results. Falkiner Fine Papers also sell a similar adhesive (WS1650). These glues can be applied to the sheet of paper using a fine airbrush.

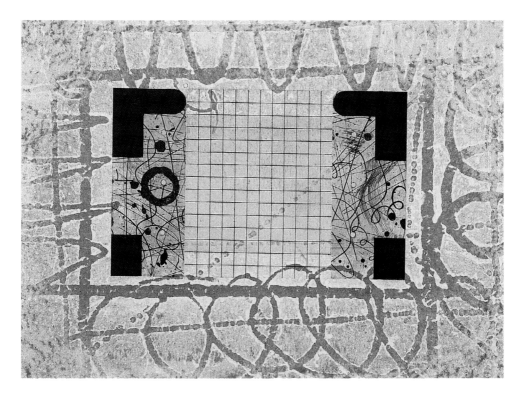

Laurence Barker, etching on handmade paper, 58 x 80 cm (23 x 31 in.).

Some thin papers may be sized for use with chine collé using rice paste, potato starch or dextrin. The following is a traditional recipe for rice-paste size from the *Tamarind Book of Lithography*:

Recipe for rice-paste size

(reproduced from the *Tamarind Book of Lithography*, courtesy of Marje Devon, Director, Tamarind Institute of Lithography, University of New Mexico, USA):

    1 part rice-paste flour
    16 parts water
    A few drops of oil of cloves to prevent souring

Heat a little of the water and gradually add the flour while stirring continuously. Keep adding the water and stirring until the mixture has dissolved, so that no lumps form. Add oil of cloves. Brush each sheet of collé paper with a soft brush on one side only. Hang up to dry or, if too fragile, place

on a piece of glass or aluminium foil. Add a few drops of glycerine if the
paper curls up too much.

WATER-LEAF (UNSIZED) PAPER

The rough side of the sheet will render different results from those you'll
obtain with the smooth side. Japanese woodblock prints will print better
on the smooth side.

TRIED AND TESTED HANDMADE PAPERS

The following information was gathered from artists across the USA who
combine handmade papers with print.

Lithography

Megan Moorhouse of Dieu Donné Papermill, New York City:
I have made all sorts of paper for lithography: 100% cotton, 100%
abaca, and combination papers of cotton plus flax or linen or abaca.
Generally speaking, I find that cotton works best for all print
processes. However, it is limited in appearance, so often we will work
with papers that are not ideal to achieve the desired look. Paper is
sized internally using Hercon 70 internal size, and we generally use
one cup of size per 10 lb of pulp.

John Risseeuw, Professor of Art, Arizona State University, Tempe:
My recipe for paper is a blend of cotton rag for strength, cotton linter,
and recycled rag mat board (10% to 15%). The mat board fibres are
very short and serve to fill in the spaces between the longer fibres,
creating a denser sheet with fewer inconsistencies in thickness. This
makes a sheet that prints better lithographically. For light sizing, I use
approximately 30–50 ml of size per 20 l of beaten pulp.

Peggy Prentice, Professor, University of Oregon:
I have made paper with 50% cotton rag and 50% cotton for lithography, sizing sheets internally with Twinrocker sizing (see list of
Suppliers, p.141) – 10 ml of size per lb of fibre. Oil- and watercolour-
based inks both worked well for the printing.

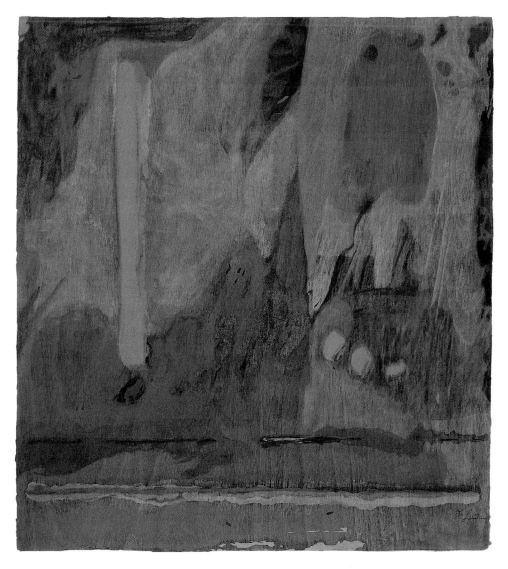

Helen Frankenthaler; *Tales of Genji III*; 1998; Woodcut; 47 x 42 in.; © Helen Frankenthaler/Tyler Graphics Ltd.

Screenprinting

Megan Moorhouse of Dieu Donné Papermill, New York City:

I usually use 100% cotton linters to screenprint on. I also recently did a project with artist Jackie Battenfield, which was printed (using water-based inks) by the Lower East Side Printshop (New York City) on 100% translucent abaca, with pulp painting on top. It was very difficult for them to print on, because the paper doesn't react well to moisture; but I believe that they sprayed it with a coating to seal it before printing. The paper was sized internally with Hercon 70 internal size.

Georgia Deal, Professor of Art, Corcoran College of Art, Washington DC:
I made a combination of abaca and cotton paper for screenprinting on, internally sized: one capful of size added to 1 lb of beaten pulp. I used TWGraphics water-based screenprinting inks to print with, which have worked well on the many occasions I have printed on my handmade papers.

Etching

Selection of paper and the type of ink used in the production of an etching is a prime consideration for the printmaker/etcher, as this means of graphic expression is often chosen specifically with tactile qualities in mind. Types of paper to experiment with include cotton, linen, abaca, and plant paper,

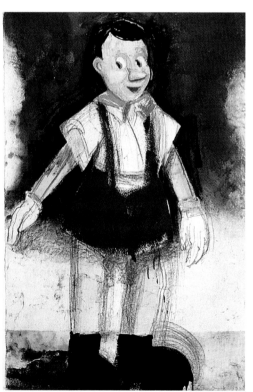

e.g., monbretia or nettle. Sizing should generally be internal, although surface sizing can sometimes be used.

Japanese *nacre* paper and *gampi* silk tissue, when used in *chine collé* mode, will receive ink well. However, *kozo* paper contains long fibres, which makes it unsuitable for copperplate etching: the fibres do not interact well with the ink, and the resulting print will have poor definition.

Jim Dine, *Red Pants II*. Coloured linen pulp, soft-ground etching, drypoint and hand-colouring, 142 x 88 cm (55¾ x 34¾ in.) 1999. Printed at/by: Dieu Donné Papermill and Pace Editions Inc. Published by Pace Editions, Inc.

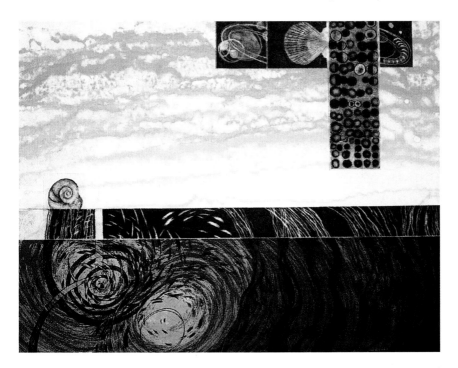

Peggy Prentice, *Nothing but the Whirling*. Etching on handmade coloured-
cotton rag. 46 x 61 cm (18 x 24 in.), 2004.

Georgia Deal, Professor of Art, Corcoran College of Art, Washington DC:
I have made paper for etching that was a combination of cotton and
abaca. This was sized internally using products from Carriage House
Press and Lee MacDonald (both USA – see List of Suppliers). I
generally use one capful of size diluted into 1 lb of beaten pulp. This
paper performed very well with oil-based inks. I have also occasionally
printed etchings on unsized sheets.

Peggy Prentice, Professor, University of Oregon:
For etching, I use 50% cotton with 50% rag, and 50% cotton linter or
rag with 50% abaca. Using 100% abaca works well if there's plenty of
soaking time prior to printing, but, if beaten for two to three hours, it
will produce a very hard, crisp sheet. I also make *amate* paper from
kozo. This can be used for etching, but needs to be dampened in a
damp pack prior to printing. For sizing, I always use Twinrocker's
internal sizing. I find that the oil-based inks perform very well on these
papers, and I wouldn't recommend printing with water-based inks.

Relief-printing: oil-based ink

Notwithstanding the mode of printing – for example, from a Columbian or Albion press, from an etching press, with wooden spoon or baren (Japanese cylindrical burnisher) – the printing problems will generally be the same. Historically, artists such as German Expressionist Ludwig Kirchner tended to use highly absorbent paper for printing; indeed, most of the Expressionists used a type of blotting paper for their prints. This could be dampened prior to printing for maximum absorbency of the ink.

Megan Moorhouse, Dieu Donné Papermill, New York City:
I have printed on sheets that are 100% cotton linters. They take the impression best. But we've also done letterpress printing on translucent abaca for a recent project with artist Elena del Rivero. The surface is not the most receptive to ink, but Swayspace (the printers) worked hard to tweak the printing so that it would be fairly consistent. The sheets were sized with Hercon 70 internal size.

John Risseeuw, Professor of Art, Arizona State University, Tempe:
To make paper for relief-printing I have used cotton rag (old clothes), cotton linter and cotton half-stuff, as well as plant fibres like sisal, jute, abaca, esparto, kapok and lots of others, usually in blends, often with cotton. I've also used recycled paper currency. I've made dozens (perhaps hundreds) of paper batches over the years for relief-printing with various combinations of fibres, most often starting with a cotton-rag base and including plant fibres that have been boiled in caustic soda and rinsed. Many editions were large enough that multiple-beater batches were necessary. Consequently, whole batches of rag or plant or linter would be beaten separately, then blended together to get the stock pulp for the vat. The advantage is that each fibre is beaten in a homogenous group for optimum beating. I nearly always lightly size handmade papers for relief-printing with Twinrocker internal sizing, which I believe is Hercon 40. The paper performed beautifully when printed on with oil-based ink. Occasionally, I have used unsized sheets to print on.

Peggy Prentice, Professor, University of Oregon:
I have used 50% cotton linter with 50% cotton rag for relief-printing, as well as 100% cotton linter, with Twinrocker's sizing in the sheets. *Moku-hanga* printing (Japanese woodblock printing using water-based

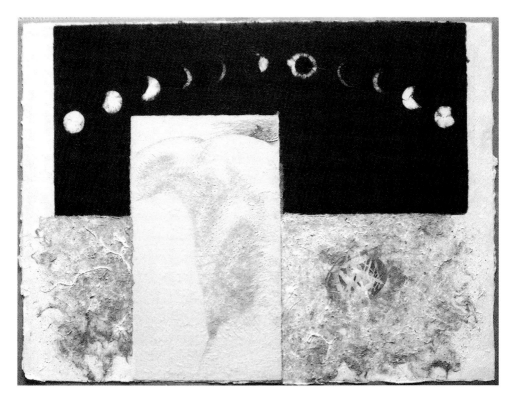

Peter Lazarov, *Eclipse*, 2003. Watermarked *kozo* pulp, Japanese woodblock print.

inks) works very well with this paper. Oil-based inks also perform very well. I sometimes print relief-and-oil monotype on unsized sheets.

Japanese woodblock printing (*mokuhan*)

Printing with water-based inks/watercolour paint.

Making your own paper for watercolour woodcuts

Freshly made Japanese paper is referred to as *kigami*. It is too weak to print on in this state: if you attempt to print on it the water-based ink will bleed and feather out from the image. Unsized paper is also fragile and will not withstand the abrasive action of the baren printing tool, which will damage the surface. However, *Jukushi*, paper strong enough to withstand several layers of print, does contain sizing or *dosa*. *Dosa* contains both alum and animal glue. When the sheet is surface-sized on both sides, it strengthens the fibres of the paper and prevents the water-based colour from blotting. The strength of the size used in sheet production deter-

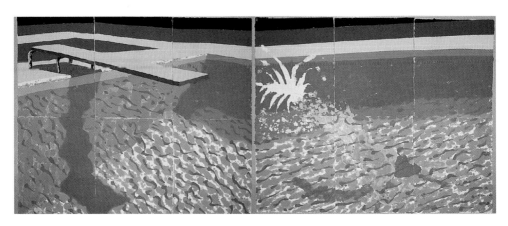

David Hockney; *Paper Pool#17 – A Diver*; 1978; coloured, pressed paper pulp; 72 x 171 in.; © David Hockney/Tyler Graphics Ltd. 1978.

mines the absorbency of the paper, which should be both absorbent and strong. The strength allows the printer to rub the sheet with the baren throughout many overprintings, without damaging it. *Kozo* (*Broussonetia kazinoki*) is the most common raw material used for papermaking in Japan. *Mitsumata* (*Edgeworthia papyrifera*) is less commonly used, and *gampi* (*Diplomorpha sikokiana*) has to be gathered in the wild.

Recipe for dosa size

The amount of *dosa* one applies to the sheet is determined by the thickness, surface and type of the paper. *Dosa* size sold in sticks is available from suppliers of Japanese art materials, and is called *sanzembon*.

A general guide for sizing high-grade *kozo* paper is as follows:

Heat one litre of water until warm. Add two *sanzembon* sticks, roughly 15–20 g, until dissolved. Add 4–6 g of alum and dissolve. Apply the solution, while still warm, to the paper sheet using a wide, soft glue brush, or something equivalent. This requires a certain skill, so keep the application light and try not to oversaturate the sheet. Starting at one end of the paper, apply the size over the sheet, using long, light strokes. Allow the sheet to dry thoroughly, preferably by pegging it to a rigged-up washing line. Then repeat the procedure on the other side of the sheet.

Paper should be sized well in advance of printing. Ideally, the paper should be left for 12 months before being printed on, as this makes the fibres crisp.

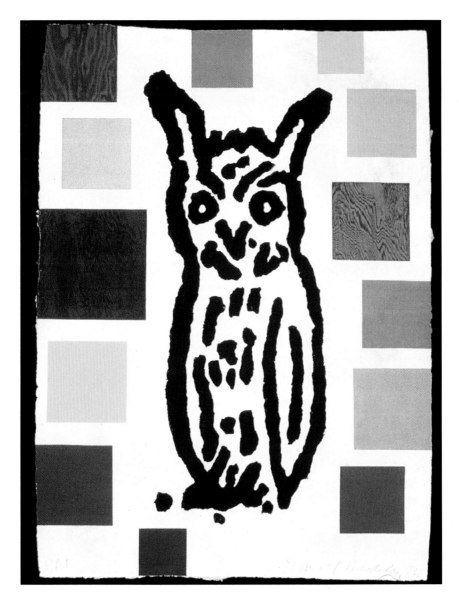

Donald Baechler, *Abstract Composition with Bird III*, 1999. 88 x 62 cm (34½ x 24½ in.); handmade paper and woodcut. Printed at/by Dieu Donné Papermill and Pace Editions Ink. Published by Pace Editions, Inc.

8 · PAPER IN THREE DIMENSIONS

by Anne Q. McKeown

Handmade paper can be used as a medium in its own right, and this chapter will show examples of paper used three-dimensionally.

Paper can be used sculpturally in many different ways. Working in their studios and hand-paper mills, visual artists can produce paper as both a unique piece and an edition. In collaborative arrangements with master papermakers, artists are introduced to the possibility of working with what to them may be a new medium. When work is planned as an edition, a print element can complete it.

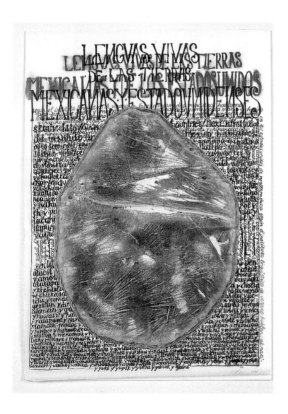

CAST PAPER

In 2000, a project began involving Laura Anderson Barbata, a New York City artist born in Mexico, in collaboration with Gail Deery, papermaker at RCIPP. Barbata's work *Ni todos los que son están, ni todos que están son* 2001 (left) is a naming of all the indigenous languages of Mexico and the United States. This list was written by Barbata in 17th-century calligraphy, and was printed with a photolithographic process in red-brown ink on the front and back of

Laura Anderson Barbata; *Ni todos los que son están, ni todos que están son*; lithograph, handmade cast abaca, *gampi* paper, lithography, push pins; 56 x 76 cm (22 x 30 in.); 2001.

a manufactured piece of highly transparent 32 x 25-inch silk tissue. This print acted as a backdrop for a handmade translucent sheet of overbeaten abaca pulp. After the abaca sheet was formed and pressed at half the usual pressure, the wet sheet was cut into an oval shape. The oval sheet was pressed again on top of a synthetic rubber casting from a mould made from the top of a cross section of a tree trunk. During pressing, foam rubber was used as packing on a hydraulic press. The sheet was restraint-dried on top of the casting, which was kept in place by the foam packing. Barbata used the section of tree trunk as a metaphor for lost languages, referring to the fact that the growth-recording rings of the tree are not revealed until the tree is cut down.

The print was mounted to a backing board, allowing the bottom of the silk tissue to hang free. The abaca paper cast was fixed to the print and the backing board with mapping pins. The number of pins used highlighted nine of the most

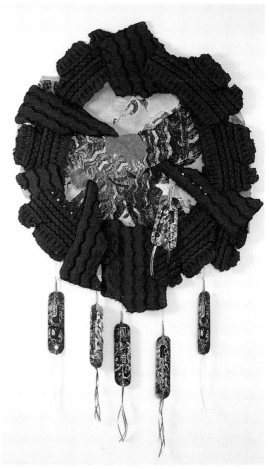

Corwin (Corky) Claremont; *Split War Shield*; cast handmade paper, lithograph, 178 x 119.5 cm (70 x 47 in.), 2001. Collaborating master papermaker: Gail Deedy.

widely spoken native languages of the USA, thirteen of the most widely spoken native languages of Mexico and three 'border-free' languages.

For the project *Split War Shield* (2001) (above), Corwin (Corky) Claremont brought truck tyres from his home at the Salish and Kootenai Indian Reservation in Montana to New Brunswick, New Jersey, to be used for a collaborative project, again with Gail Deery. This art work relates to the US Government's intention to build a truck route directly through the land of the Salish and Kootenai Indian Reservation. Two pieces of hand-made paper contain embedded photographic images of the Montana landscape, printed with lithographic images of symbols. Large, cast black pieces of cotton paper imprinted with the tyre treads encircle the print. Synthetic rubber was used to cast moulds directly from the Montana tyres. Black-denim cotton pulp was prepared, applied wet to the moulds and air-dried. The cotton fibre was long, and did not have much shrinkage rate, so the pulp did not have to be restrained while it dried.

Ethan Shoshan's work, entitled *He simply walked into the bedroom with her and, trembling with desire, slowly slipped off her clothes. And in the soft light of twilight, with the music of the foghorns bleating softly in the distance, they made love.* (2001) (below), demonstrates the use of cast paper as an art work. Shoshan seeks out old paperback romantic novels, removes the covers, tears up the pages and cuts out certain phrases and words; these are put aside. The pages are then saturated with water and put into a Hollander beater, which returns them to pulp. Certain other pulps will be added to the original pages to affect colour and increase the binding strength. When the pages have been sufficiently pulped, the extracted phrases and words are added, embedded in the prepared pulp but still clearly legible. The pulp is placed into plaster moulds where it is air-dried. There is no restraint mechanism to hold the pulp in the predetermined

Ethan Shoshan, *He simply walked into the bedroom with her and, trembling with desire, slowly slipped off her clothes. And in the soft light of twilight, with the music of the foghorns bleating softly in the distance, they made love.* Cast books on wooden tables, 244 x 366 cm (96 x 144 in.), 2001.

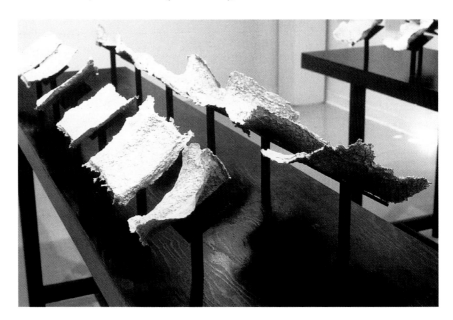

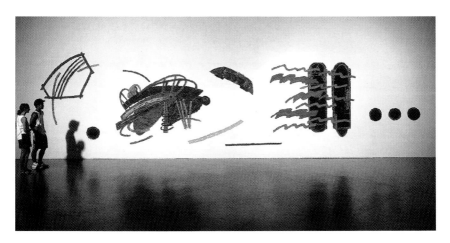

Joan Hall, *Debris*. Shaped handmade paper, pulp painting, printed elements, 3 x 9 m (10 x 30 ft), 1991. Courtesy of Elliot Smith Contemporary Art.

shape of the mould. As the pulp dries it tends to bend and twist – to cockle. This cockling is used to exaggerate the liveliness of the object, by emulating the 'heat' of the words in the novels. A number of 'books' were made for this project, displayed on specially built book stands. These were fixed to tables, which are meant to refer to tall library tables.

BUILDING LARGE WORK

Eve Ingalls uses different pulps to build her sculptural constructions. The pulp is applied to the armature in the form of sheets made from handfuls of pulp and cooked, beaten and unbeaten strips of the inner bark of the paper mulberry tree. The inside and outside surfaces of the paper are well considered, so that the forms exist fully in space, and the observer finds the surface shifting and changing from every viewpoint. Steel rods are used to reinforce and support the shaped pieces. Ingalls's paper work, entitled *From/Since* (2002) (see p.112), is an example of the scale that can be achieved within the medium of paper. Paper is lightweight, and with the appropriate preparation it has great strength. In her studio, Ingalls applied cooked mulberry bark to moulds for casting, as well as directly to the sculpture. Cast abaca, tea, pigment, yarn and metal are all elements within this piece. Previously, Eve has built sculpture on many varied supports. Perhaps the most unique process was to build images on the charred remains of huge tree trunks – remnants of the devastating forest fires of 2002 in the Bitterroot Mountains of northern Idaho.

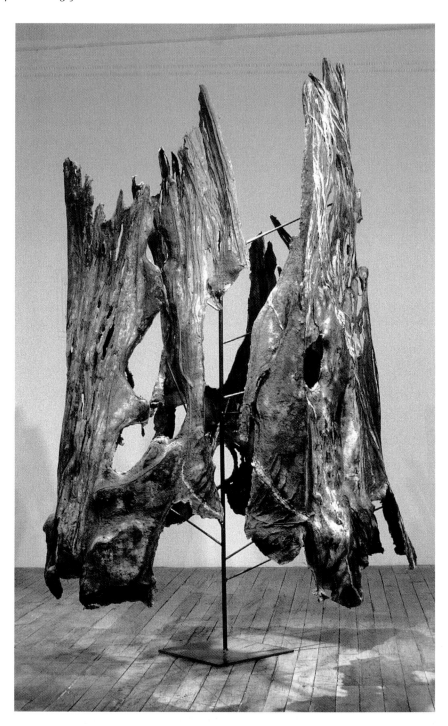

Eve Ingalls, *From/Since*. Pigmented abaca, metal rods;
254 x 142 x 132 cm (100 x 56 x 52 in.), 2002.

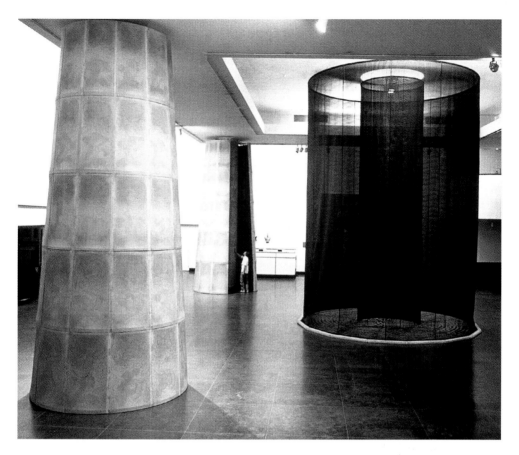

Winifred Lutz, *Ago/Anon.* Flax paper, wood, sand, Mylar™, screening material, limestone blocks. 8.5 x 18.3 x 24.4 m (28 x 60 x 80 ft); 1990.

Winifred Lutz also works on large-scale paper installations. *Ago/Anon*
(1990) (above) was installed in the grand lobby of the Brooklyn Museum
in New York, in a space 28 feet high by 60 feet wide by 80 feet deep. This
installation, which consisted of a set of massive columns, was constructed
from handmade overbeaten flax paper, wood, black tent screening,
Mylar™ and sand.

Throughout her career, Joan Hall has constructed enormous works in
handmade paper, building numerous presses, vats, moulds and drying
systems for this purpose. For *Debris* (1991) (see p.111), after making drawings to scale, the individual pieces were hand-formed on a vacuum table.
The pulp ingredients, in this case cotton and abaca, were beaten together
in a Hollander beater. The dried paper pieces were then printed with col-
lographs and relief-printing techniques. After printing, more imagery was

developed by pulp-painting. The pieces were fastened together and fixed to the wall, the entire group measuring 10 feet high by 30 feet long.

Joan Giordano uses abaca to create voluminous but lightweight sculpture on a large scale. She participated in a fellowship at the Awagami paper mill in Tokushima, home to the Fujimori family, on the Japanese island of Shikoku. While working there she discovered the strength and beauty of abaca fibre, and with this new-found information she returned to New York to develop her own work. In her paper work *Time and the River* (2001) (below), ribbons of mesh bond the abaca fibre, which is formed above and below the mesh, then vacuumed on a powerful vacuum table to draw water out of the pulp. The fibre and mesh air-dry to a certain dampness, whereupon it is pounded with a metal scraper. This pounding binds the fibres and mesh together, also rendering it with a textured surface.

Joan Giordano, *Time and the River*, abaca, wire mesh, aluminium. 152 x 152 x 20 cm (60 x 60 x 8 in.), 2001.

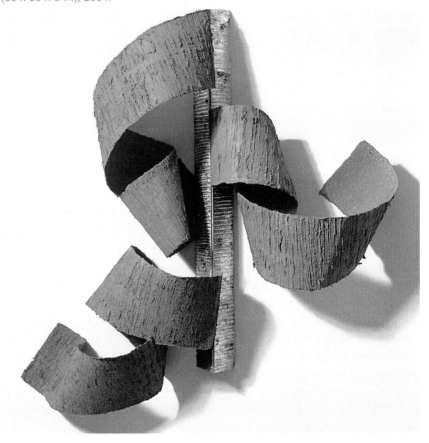

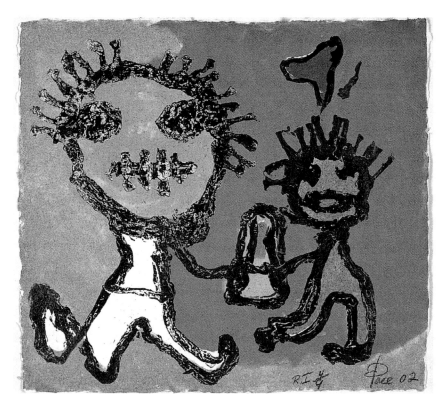

Lorenzo Pace, *Jalani no. 8.*, handmade paper, pulp painting. 32 x 35 cm (12½ x 13¾ in.), 2002. Collaborating master papermaker: Anne Q. McKeown.

PULP PAINTING

Lorenzo Pace was interested in collaborating with me at RCIPP to rework images from his published children's book *Jalani* at RCIPP. The images for this project were narrowed down to eight, and a method was sought to maintain the quality of the original drawings. Brilliant colour was also a consideration for the project; this type of colour is easy to achieve with receptive, overbeaten fibres of linen rag.

Because of the inherent properties of *kozo*, which is wonderfully pliable after it is cooked and also strong once it dries, it was deemed the best pulp for Lorenzo to use in drawing the characters for each of the images, such as *Jalani no. 8* (2002) (above). Where the strips were overlapping they were pounded with a hard object to fuse them. Once dried, they were coated with an acrylic medium to prevent the fibre from pulling apart as they were inked and printed during editioning. These drawings were the key

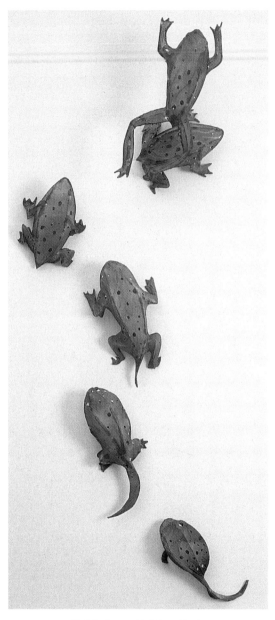

Christy Rupp, *Moisture Seekers*, 1996/2000, steel covered with water-marked, pigmented abaca paper. Variable sizes, approximately 40.5 x 30.5 x 12.5 cm (16 x 12 x 5 in.) each. Collaborating master papermakers: Paul Wong and Pat Almonronde. Courtesy of the artist and Dieu Donne Papermill.

matrix, completed first. They acted as guides for the stencils used to add layers of colour (pigmented pulp paint) to the wet paper. Stencils made from dressmakers' interfacing were cut for each *Jalani* image, one for each colour. Each wet stencil was laid down on a freshly made sheet of abaca paper measuring 33 x 35.5 cm (13 x 14 in.). The pigmented, overbeaten pulp was applied through squeeze bottles to the cut-out areas, one colour at a time. Once the paper and the pulp paint dried, each *kozo* matrix was inked in black relief ink and printed onto the stencilled, handmade paper.

SHEET FORMATION AND ARMATURES

Christy Rupp, whose work is concerned with ecological themes, comments on the fragility of ecological systems through her recreation of frogs.

She uses the translucency of overbeaten, watermarked, pigmented abaca to capture the surface beauty of these amphibians. In *Moisture Seekers* (2001) (left) Rupp worked in collaboration with Paul Wong and Pat Almonrode at Dieu Donné Papermill. Rupp prepared a welded-iron skeleton of the object she wished to portray, to which previously pulled and pressed wet sheets were attached.

Methylcellulose was applied to the edges of the paper, which were folded over the metal rods and attached to the body of wet paper, which in turn became taut on the skeleton as it dried. This process needed to be finely anticipated: if the wet paper had been too snug when it was fixed to the skeleton, it could have become too taut during drying and burst, ripping the paper. Finally, areas of the skeleton were left open to enable light to pass through the overbeaten translucent paper, and burn holes were added to the surface.

Lynda Benglis worked with Megan Moorehouse at Dieu Donné to make her sculptures, which resemble body parts. In *Brother Animals* (2001) (right) and *Earth Cavern* (2001) (below) a thin coil of aluminium wire was firstly wrapped around a tube in a spiral formation. Short-fibred, translucent abaca was pigmented a pinky-flesh colour. From this, paper sheets were formed, pressed and rolled

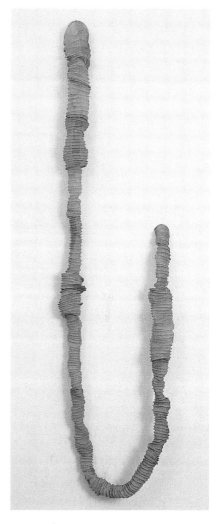

Lynda Benglis. RIGHT *Brother Animals*, aluminium wire coils covered with translucent abaca paper, pigment, gold leaf. 10 x 264 cm (4 x 104 in.), 2001.
BELOW *Earth Cavern*, aluminium wire coils covered with translucent abaca paper, pigment, gold leaf. 18 x 107 cm (7 x 42 in.), 2001. Collaborating master papermaker (both pieces): Megan Moorhouse. Courtesy of the artists and Dieu Donné Papermill.

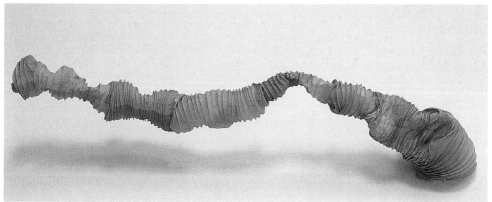

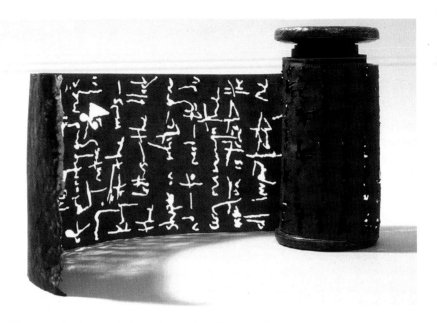

Robbin Ami Silverberg, *Black Torah*. Graphite, flax, wood; 2003.

around the wire and joined together with methylcellulose to make a tube of flesh-coloured paper. The paper and wire were then pulled off the tube in one piece, the pink translucent tubes being allowed to air-dry. As the paper dried, the fibre shrinkage encased the wire, rendering the paper tubes increasingly flexible.

TRANSLUCENCY

Simulacrum (2003) (page 122) is an installation of nine lean-to forms, each measuring 107 x 61 cm (42 x 24 in.), by Robbin Ami Silverberg. Pulp paint and cut shapes enliven the translucent abaca paper, which is attached to glass forms, allowing maximum translucency and visibility of the pulp-painted imagery. On both sides of the abaca paper, paper pulp records oral histories from the Jewish Women's Archive of women born in the early 20th century.

Silverberg also makes small editions of artist's books at Dobbin Mill in Brooklyn, New York in collaboration with other artists. One of Robbin's own unique artist's books is called *Black Torah* (2003) (above). The flax pulp has been pigmented a deep graphite. The paper, 335 cm (132 in.) long, was attached to a wood and metal spool. Hebrew characters were deliberately burned out of the black paper to create a negative space.

EMBEDDED WIRE

Chakaia Booker, who uses tyres and inner tubes in her work, collabrated with me at RCIPP on the following piece. The paper for *Visual Impression II* (2002) (right), required to mimic the mass and 'bounce' of rubber, was arrived at using the following method:

A skeleton of wire was attached to the paper pieces. The base structure was formed with pierced holes in the formed sheet. To reinforce the structure, and render the paper able to move in space, pieces of wire were firstly wrapped with string and pulled through a vat of lengthy brown-black abaca pulp. This pulp-looped wire was placed onto the wet

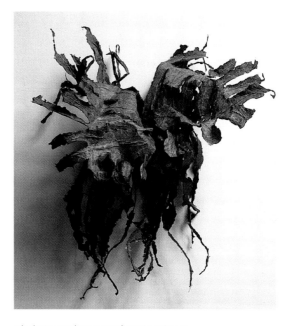

Chakaia Booker, *Visual Impression II*, 2002. Collaborating master papermaker: Anne Q. McKeown. Courtesy of RCIPP.

sheets, and, when the sheet and the looped pulp dried, they were attached. After the top and bottom forms had been attached and dried, two mirror images were stitched together. Once the piece had been assembled, both sides of the pigmented abaca were sprayed with water. Booker then manipulated the dampened paper so that it opened up as much as possible.

ASSEMBLAGE

Leslie Dill has worked on collaborative projects at Dieu Donné Papermill in New York City. With Annie Murdock, Dill created her *Paper Poem Dress* (*The Thrill Came Slowly like a Boon, E.D.*) (1995) (see p.120, top). Linen paper was laminated onto sections of wire to construct a tall dress. Wire, formed to the shape of a written line of poetry by Emily Dickinson, was dipped in paper pulp and then draped around the dress, thereby wrapping it in words. In 2003 Dill, in collaboration with Jan Drojarski and Paul Wong, created her paper work *Head* (page 120, below). This powerful though small work, a mere six inches tall, is made of pigmented, die-cut abaca. The resultant paper letters are assembled over a mould to form the head, and threads fall from the eyes.

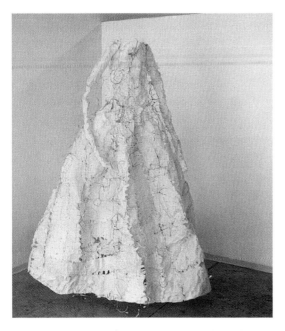

Lynne Allen employs hand-made paper as an element within her printed and constructed paper objects. For *Moccasins #2* (2002) (opposite) she began by making a newly formed handmade paper sheet to which a stencilled image made from pigmented, overbeaten pulp was added. (Stencils can be made from many different mediums: Mylar (acetate), dress-makers' interfacing, puff paint (textured fabric paint), etc.) After the paper was dried the imagery was further developed with an imprint from an etched plate, after which the paper was cut and re-formed, and the paper 'moccasins' were covered in shellac.

R.G. Brown worked at RCIPP with me to create *Journey Series – Lost Memories* (2004) (see p.123). This piece comprised 35 over-beaten abaca sheets, each 71 x 96.5 cm (28 x 38 in.). At his studio Brown made a skeleton of a boat from white cedar, which he

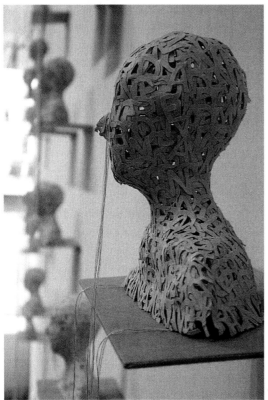

Lesley Dill TOP *Paper Poem Dress (The Thrill Came Slowly like a Boon, E.D.)*, 1995. Wire, linen, handmade paper, 228.5 x 172.5 x 96.5 cm (90 x 68 x 38 in.). Images courtesy of the artist, Dieu Donné Papermill, and George Adams Gallery, New York.

LEFT *Head*, 2003. Cast die-cut, pigmented abaca paper letters, thread. 15 cm (6 in.) high. Images courtesy of the artist, Dieu Donné Papermill and George Adams Gallery, New York.

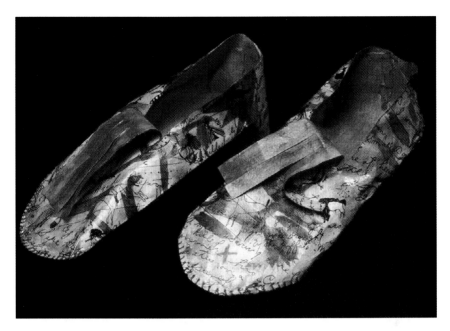

Lynne Allen, *Moccasins #2*, 2002. Linen/cotton handmade paper, stencilled pulp paint, etched paper, thread.

covered with these abaca sheets, which in turn he subsequently waxed. Two fresh sheets were couched together with lengths of tubular grass trapped between them.

YARN AND WIRE GRIDS AS MATRIX

Wire grids, vibrant colour, drawing in space and a playful element are components in Alan Shields's sculpture. Shields's work consists of techniques that use pulp in creative, non-traditional processes. At Dieu Donné, Shields collaborated with Pat Almonrode on *Bee Bee Waiting* (2002) and with both Pat and Lee Running on *Monkey Cage Cow* (2002) (page 129). Both pieces were painted with watercolour to pigment the paper after the pieces were dry. The painted surface creates a different effect with the inclusion of pigment in the pulp. The translucency of the watercolour and the reflective power of the white cotton fibre creates lively colour.

(Note that rather than adding aqueous dispersed pigment to pulp to achieve colour, some artists use rag that has already been dyed. Some colours – e.g. deep red and intense black – are difficult to achieve by just adding pigment.)

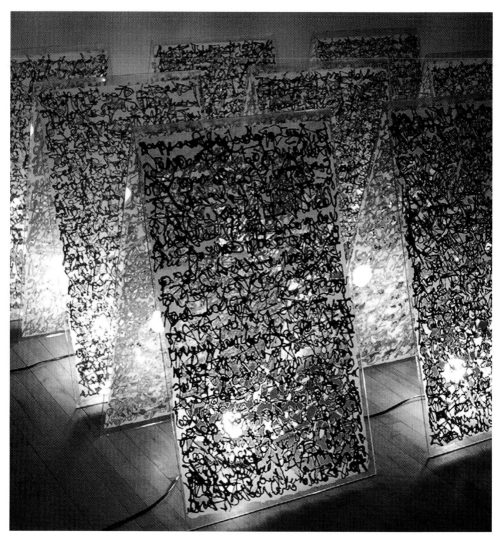

Robbin Ami Silverberg, *Simulacrum*. Pulp painting, translucent abaca, glass, each 107 x 61 cm (42 x 24 in.), 2003.

BLOWOUTS (LACE STENCIL OR MOYOGAMI)

With Western paper formation a 'blowout' usually uses very short, pigmented pulp. The blowout process is similar to a Japanese paper process that uses jets of water to pierce and rearrange wet *kozo* that has been formed into a sheet. The most well-known paper to use this process is called 'lace paper'.

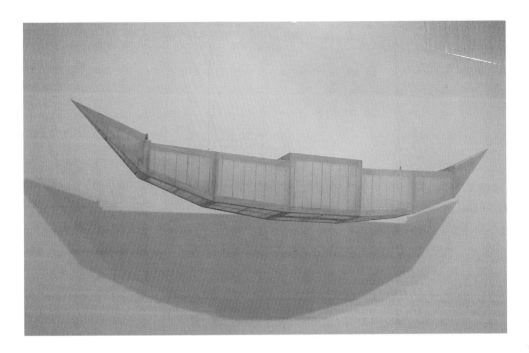

R.G. Brown, *Journey Series – Lost Memories*. Abaca paper, cedar, 350 x 45.5 x 73.5 cm (138 x 18 x 29 in.), 2004.

Eve Ingalls used a pulp blowout when collaborating with me on her paper work *Fingering Instability* (2002) (page 124), in which she cut out foam-sheet stencils in the shape of her image. A fresh sheet of heavily pigmented abaca was pulled and kept on the mould. The foam shapes were placed one by one on the fresh sheet of paper, then a heavy stream of water was used to 'blow away' the pulp in the non-image area. The sheet of paper then became the shape of the foam sheet, the edges irregular and more organic than the deckles of a cast, shaped sheet. The six image-shaped sheets were placed in two rows on plastic boards. Lengths of yarn were pulled through a vat to catch pulp, then placed on the fresh sheets of paper to connect all six together. Ingalls designed metal rods from which to hang the paper work, so that shadows created by this hanging system form an integral part of the piece.

Sculptor Nancy Cohen's *Reticular Hammock* (2002) (see p.126) was made using paper dried on monofilament and assembled with wax. The entire piece is hung from a glass support. Cohen has found countless ways of incorporating paper into her sculptures, and in these works paper is combined with found pieces as well as the crafted glass elements that are built around the paper.

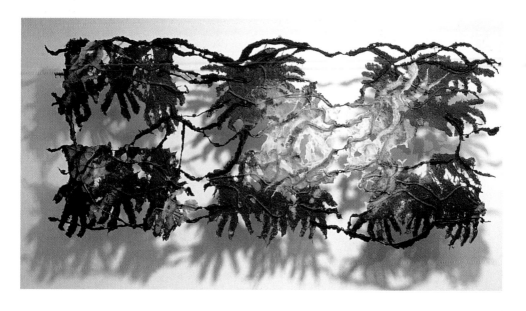

Eve Ingalls, *Fingering Instability*. Cast paper, yarn; 68.5 x 147.5 x 14 cm
(27 x 58 x 5½ in.), 2002.

PAPER IN MIXED MEDIA AND INSTALLATION

Dianne Reeves collects found objects; bones and boxes are components in
her work. Paper's ability to form almost any shape is an important consideration in her method. *Seizing Penumbra* (1996) (see p.127) is made from
dried abaca paper, cow ribs, test tubes, casing, alligator feet, cicada shells,
beaver claws, gauze, gesso and PVA glue.

Marilyn Sward's installation *Directional Energy* (1999) (see p.126) is 12 m
(40 ft) in diameter. It is composed of eight sculptures six to eight feet tall,
which stand at the directional points found on a compass. The colours of the
sculptures refer to directions relating to Native American legends; the sculptures themselves are made of hand-formed, dried abaca sheets. The sheets
are attached to cardboard and foam core, and after completion the forms are
painted with polyurethane to withstand adverse weather conditions.

PAPER FOR DIGITAL PRINT

Enrique Leal, who worked at RCIPP as a visiting artist, is a professor in the
print department of the University of Castilla-La Mancha in Cuenca, Spain.

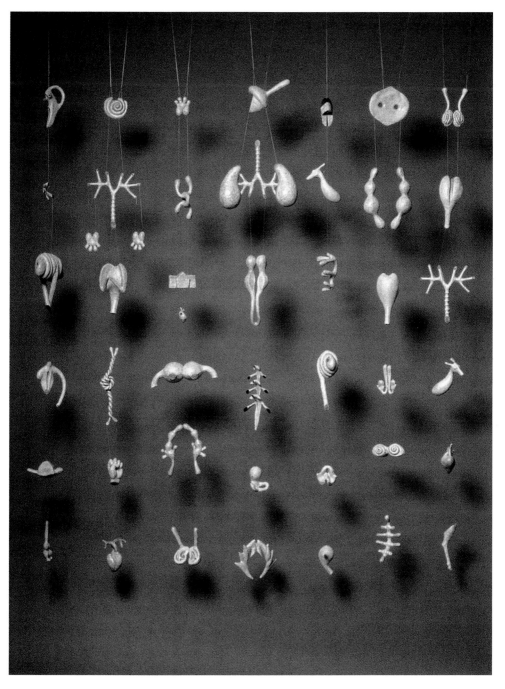

Jeanne Jaffe, *Spill of Memory*, 1998. 244 x 305 x 25 cm (96 x 120 x 10 in.); paper.

RIGHT Marilyn Sward, *Directional Energy*, 1999. Handformed dried abaca sheets, card, foam. 12 x 1.8 x 2.4 m (40 x 6 x 8 ft).

BELOW LEFT Nancy Cohen, *Reticular Hammock*, 2002. Cement, handmade paper, glass, string, acrylic, 30.5 x 13 x 18 cm (12 x 5 x 7 in.).

BELOW RIGHT Dianne Reeves, *Seizing Penumbra*, 1996. Dyed abaca paper, mixed media, 32 x 76 x 38 cm (12½ x 30 x 15 in.)

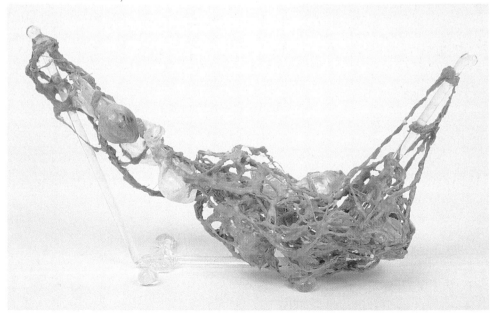

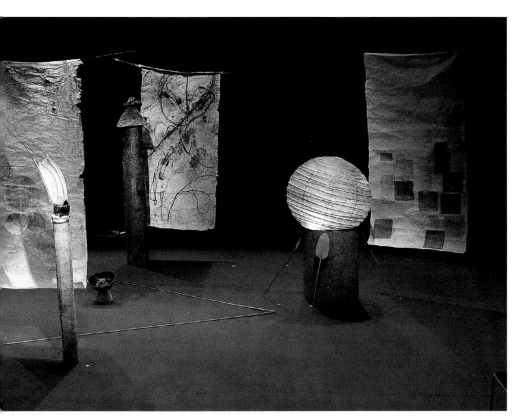

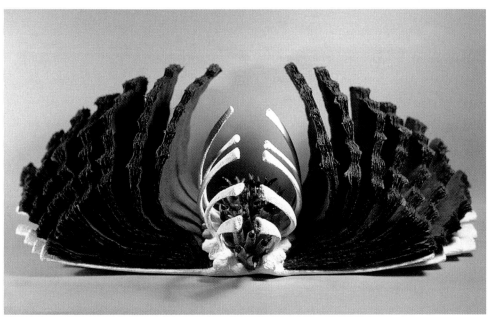

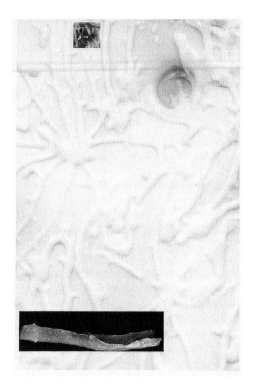

Enrique Leal, *Olho(s) III*, 2004. Handmade bleached hemp, digital print.

He works with handmade paper to build objects that record the intricate designs produced by the tunnelling action of beetles upon branches. First of all he makes synthetic rubber moulds of the branches. Then he forms sheets of over-beaten, bleached hemp, which he lays over them. In order to maintain in the paper object the tunnelling designs from the wood, a synthetic rubber mould is placed over the wet paper. This mould keeps the paper from pulling away from the branch as it dries. The resulting paper sheets are very thin, thus enhancing the fibre's translucency. The thinness of the paper allows it to dry without growing mould, even though it is wrapped in synthetic rubber. Once Leal has perfected his paper object, he digitally scans it. The digital image of the paper, the synthetic rubber and the branch became the imagery Leal used to create *Olho(s) III* (2004) (left), one of the digital prints in his *Entomography* series.

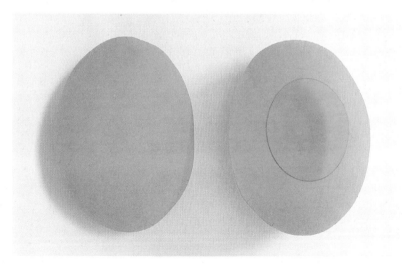

Jacki Parry, *Untitled*. Cast-paper sculpture.

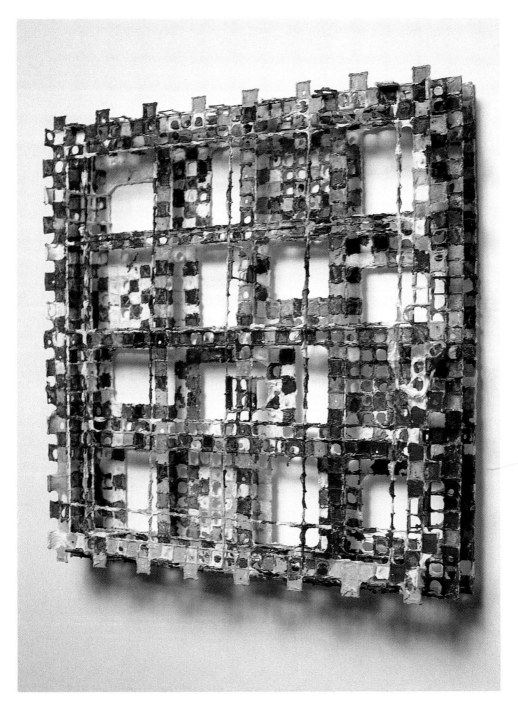

Alan Shields, *Monkey Cage Cow*, 2002. 39 x 39 x 8 cm (15½ x 15½ x 3 in.); water-colour on cotton pulp-dipped armature.

GLOSSARY

Abaca (*Musa textilis*) A Philippine plant related to the banana, also known as Manila hemp, it produces translucent, naturally buff-coloured paper. Due to its high rate of shrinkage when beaten for long periods, it is used by papermakers for sculptural techniques.

Alkali A caustic substance used in the cooking of plant fibres such as soda ash (sodium carbonate) wood-ash lye, washing soda and lime (calcium hydroxide) to remove non-cellulose materials.

Alum A complex salt, commonly potassium aluminium sulphate, added to the pulp in the beater, along with rosin sizing, when dyeing paper pulp. It confers water-resistant properties on the paper and acts as a mordant to fix colours. It can also cause irreversible deterioration of paper if used in excessive quantities. Papermaker's alum is aluminium sulphate.

Armature A supporting structure for sculpture made of wood, metal or other material.

Archival Paper A lignin-free paper with a pH value of between 6.5 and 8, it has long-lasting qualities.

Bast Fibre The soft, inner woody fibre (dicotyledons) obtained from the inner bark of many shrubs and trees – for example, *gampi*, *kozo*, *mitsumata* and certain herbaceous plants such as hemp, flax and ramie. When separated from the outer bark, remaining fibre provides a material suitable for making either paper or textiles.

Beating The mechanical or manual process of cutting, macerating, shredding or splitting the fibres or rags in water. This prepares them for hydrogen bonding, which occurs during the papermaking and drying process. Beating affects the finished result of the paper in many ways, for example, in relation to the opacity, smoothness and formation of the sheets.

Beater Beating mechanisms include the Hollander beater, a 17th-century Dutch invention still in use today. Blenders, wooden mallets (hardwood is best) and standard kitchen blenders can also be used in pulp preparation. Whiz mixers, available from papermaking suppliers, rehydrate processed pulps.

Bleaching A purification of the fibres and pulp by removing lignins, and by whitening using chlorine compounds.

Calcium Carbonate (CaCO3) This is used when sheet-forming to improve the opacity and the whiteness of the pulp. It also increases the alkaline content of the paper, and renders sheets smoother, acting as a subtle filler between fibres. It is also referred to as a buffering agent.

Calendering Passing a sheet of paper through a metal roller (as in an etching press) or direct press (as in a direct-lithographic press) to impart a smooth or glossy finish to the surface.

Cast Paper Three-dimensional paper works constructed by moulding wet pulp around a form or armature. Once dry, the paper is released from the mould and can be viewed as a sculpture or relief.

Cellulose A carbohydrate, forming the main part of plant-cell tissues. Cellulose provides the fundamental substance for paper. All living plants contain varying degrees of cellulose. Fibrous plants have a high percentage of cellulose.

Chain Lines Widely spaced lines impressed in a sheet of paper by employing a laid mould. Chain stitch is used to sew the laid wires to the ribs of the paper mould.

Chemical Cotton Cotton-linter pulp that has been produced from the shorter seed hairs of the plant, processed by cooking, bleaching and forming into sheets (see Linters).

Cooking Preparation of raw plant fibres for papermaking, usually with the aid of an alkali, although some fibres may be retted (see Retting). Cooking softens tough fibres, allowing easier beating, and removes unwanted plant material and lignins.

Cotton One of the main fibres used in Western-style papermaking. The soft white filaments of the fibre are attached to the seeds of the cotton plant. Cotton is the purest form of cellulose that occurs in nature.

Cotton Rag Any material originating from the long fibre of the cotton seed. It can also be recycled rag, for example, from 'old' cotton bed sheets or 'new' shirt or clothing cuttings from factory sources.

Couching From the French verb *coucher* (meaning in this instance 'to lie [something] down'), couching is the act of transferring a newly formed sheet of paper from the surface of the mould onto a wet felt (in Western papermaking).

Deckle The wooden frame which fits over and around the mould to contain the pulp during the dipping and forming action, preventing it from falling off the mould.

Deckle Edge The jagged, but characteristic paper edge created by the leanness of the pulp trapped underneath the deckle frame.

Deckle Box A mould with a deep deckle into which pulp is poured, a deckle box is often used when a thick sheet of paper is required.

Embedding Trapping elements within a sheet of paper, for example, by sandwiching items between two transparent sheets.

Embossing Creating a raised or depressed surface on a sheet by running it, dampened, through a press on top of an incised or built-up plate or matrix. Embossed images can be produced with or without ink, the latter process being referred to as 'blind' embossing.

Felt A heavy cloth, usually made of wool, upon which the newly formed paper sheets are couched.

Fibrillation A term which describes what happens during the beating process: the individual cellulose fibres are bruised and roughened to enable them to bond during sheet formation.

Filler Minerals – for example, calcium carbonate and titanium dioxide – are added to fibre during the beating stage to render the sheet smoother, whiter or more opaque.

Flax Fibre (*Linum usitatissimum*) The bast fibre of the plant, used in the production of both paper and linen.

Flocculation This occurs when fibres clump together as the paper sheets are being formed.

Formation Aid In its natural form, a substance used in Japanese papermaking to slow drainage during sheet-forming, thus improving distribution of fibre in the vat. In Japan, papermakers use natural formation aid, extracted from the root of the plant *tororo-aoi* (*Hibiscus manihot (L.)*). A mucous substance is taken from the crushed roots, which is referred to as *neri*. Synthetic formation aid is now available through papermaking suppliers in the USA, including PMP, PNS and PEO. Formation agents can also be made from okra and the roots of the hollyhock.

Fourdrinier A type of modern papermaking machine. This works on the principle of the continuous web machine that was invented by Frenchman Nicolas Louis Robert in 1798. The design concept was passed on to the Fourdrinier brothers in London, whose engineers improved the original design.

Gampi (*Diplomorpha sikokiana*) This is a low-growth deciduous tree of the Thymelaceae family. It is difficult to cultivate and thus is often harvested in the wild. The fibre is thin, very lustrous and short, and resilient to insects, which renders it very strong. It produces excellent paper of wonderful translucency.

Gelatin A glutinous type of protein extracted from animal tissue by boiling, it is used as an external size to render paper resistant to bleeding or staining during the print process.

Hemp Originating in Asia, it was first used to make paper in the 1st century AD. It contains a fibre of high cellulose content, which has good length and strength, and makes a paper that is white and lustrous.

Hollander Beater A machine developed in Holland that replaced the stamping mill in the latter part of the 17th century. A common piece of fibre-preparation equipment, it is used to beat rags and fibres to a pulp in preparation for papermaking. It macerates, shortens and hydrates the fibres as they pass between a roll with flat-ended blades and a bedplate.

Hydration As they are beaten, the bruised fibres begin to absorb water more easily. The hydration will reduce the opacity of the resulting paper, and increase its bonding strength, due to the water retained in the fibre.

Hydraulic Press A press that expels water by means of a vertical pressure applied to the newly formed sheets of paper as they are held in the press between felts.

Inclusions Any type of dry matter – for example, dried flowers, thread or paper – placed between thin sheets of (usually) translucent pulp.

Interfacing A polyester material sold in fabric stores, used in dressmaking. It can be used as a papermaking felt. The American equivalent is called pellon.

Jute (*Corchrus olitorius*) Native to India, this plant contains between 60 and 90 per cent pure cellulose. It was a popular fibre for papermaking in the 18th century.

Kaolin Also known as china clay, this fine white powder is added to pulp to render the paper opaque and smooth.

Kozo (*Broussonetia kazinoki*) This is a low-growth deciduous tree of the Moraceae or mulberry family. Several varieties are used in papermaking, and the fibres are long, strong and sinewy.

Laid Mould A mould consisting of a series of parallel wires or laid lines attached or sewn to ribs supported from below. Laid lines are visible on sheets of paper constructed in this way.

Lexan stencil A transparent material similar to acetate but slightly thicker.

Lignin A polymer material that supports the cellulose fibres of the woody plant by bonding them together, lignin can be dissolved by cooking the fibre in a solution of alkali. Pulp producers consider both lignin and inorganic materials that make up the plant or tree as contaminants.

Linters These resemble thick sheets of white blotting paper, and are pre-washed and boiled, having been processed in a machine called a linter. They consist of shorter fibres that remain on the cotton seed after the longer fibres have been ginned away for use in textile production.

Mitsumata (*Edgeworthia papyrifera* or *Daphne papyrifera*) This has uncertain origins, but was documented as first being used to make paper around 1597. The inner bark produces a fine-grained and lustrous paper.

Mixografia® The Mixografia technique is a unique fine art printing process that allows for the production of three-dimensional prints with texture and very fine surface detail. With this process, the artist creates a model or 'maquette' with any solid material or combination of materials on which he or she incises, impresses, carves, collages or builds-up in relief, the image to be reproduced.

Mould A basic tool in papermaking in which the sheets are formed. The surface of the mould is a screen constructed of various types of mesh, which catches the paper pulp, simultaneously letting water drain through it.

Mylar® A type of acetate used in the US for print registration.

Nagashi-zuki A literal translation is 'the flowing way to make paper'. In brief, the pulp and water are scooped onto the paper mould several times to achieve the required sheet thickness. The screen is then released from the mould, and the wet sheets are laid on top of each other edge to edge on a post.

Neri This term describes the different types of vegetable mucilage used in Japanese papermaking, such as the one extracted from the *tororo-aoi* root. This substance prevents fibres from clumping together during the sheet-forming process, and allows slow drainage.

No-See-Um netting A polyester mesh with a fine weave sold in the USA, it is a finer type of mosquito netting. It can be used in the making of a Japanese *sugeta* mould, and for transferring watermarked stencils.

Pellon A non-woven mesh of polyester made in the USA used as a surface for couching (see Interfacing).

Pigment A finely ground colouring material used to colour pulp. These pigments need to be used in conjunction with retention aid, which binds them to the fibre.

Post A group of freshly formed sheets of paper, sandwiched between felts (in Western papermaking) or stacked without felts (in Japanese papermaking).

Pulp A soft mass, derived from wood, plant fibre or rags, from which paper is formed.

Rag A type of fabric used in the papermaking process. Cotton rag contains long fibres.

Ramie Also known as China grass, rhea and grasscloth, this is classed as a cellulose fibre. One of the oldest of all vegetable fibres, it was used for Chinese burial shrouds over 2,000 years ago.

Retention Aid A cationic material which bonds pigment to the surface of fibre.

Retting A fermenting process whereby rags or plants are left to rot in order to break down the fibre content. Alkaline solutions (for example, calcium hydroxide) are often employed in the process of retting. Retting can occur when fibre is exposed to rain or dew.

Rice Paper A misnomer used to described Japanese paper (*washi*). Rice paste was sometimes used as a size in papers produced in the past, but rice alone will not make paper.

Shim Stencil A metal stencil made out of various materials, e.g., brass.

Sizing A material incorporated into the paper fibre, either during the beating process (internal sizing such as Hercon 70) or after the sheet has been dried (surface sizing). This controls both the subsequent damping of the sheet and the way in which the paper surface accepts the printing ink. Sizing renders the paper more water-repellent.

Stuff Concentrated beaten fibre or pulp before it has been mixed with other materials in order to make paper.

Sugeta The name for the Japanese papermaking mould, which consists of the *su*, a removable bamboo screen, and the *keta*, a hinged frame.

Tamezuki This translates as 'fibre-settling papermaking method' and is the Japanese term for Western papermaking – that is, one pull from the vat, felts between the newly formed sheets, and initial heavy pressing.

Wove This term refers to a mould surface constructed of woven screen. This mould is used to make paper with a consistent surface that does not contain laid or chain lines.

PREPARING A STANDARD ALKALI SOLUTION FROM WOOD ASH

This extract is taken from Maureen Richardson's book Handmade Paper *(Apple Press), with the permission of the author.*

1. Lye made from wood ash (potassium carbonate) makes a standard alkali solution. Perforate the base of a plastic bucket and line it with 8 layers of plastic net. Place it inside another bucket to catch the drained liquid (this should not reach right to the bottom of the first bucket). Pierce 2 sharp sticks through the top of the net bag, and balance them on the rim of the second bucket. It will look a little like a jelly bag. Pour 3 lbs (1.35kg) dry weight of wood ash into the net bag.

2. Pour 12 pints (6.8 l) of boiling water over the ash - you do not have to pour all the water in at the same time, but can continue to refill and boil the kettle.

3. When all the water has drained through and cooled down, take a pH reading from the liquid in the lower bucket. It should be somewhere between 9 and 12.

NB: Stout waterproof gloves, face mask, and goggles are recommended for safety whenever you are working with alkali solutions.

BIBLIOGRAPHY

Adams, Clinton & Antreasian, Garo, *The Tamarind Book of Lithography: Art & Techniques*, New York, Harry N. Abrams, Inc. Publishers, 1971. (ISBN 8109-9017-2)

Awa Japanese Handmade Paper (pamphlet), Tokushima, Awa Handmade Japanese Paper Industrial Cooperative.

Barrett, Timothy, *Japanese Papermaking: Tradition, Tools and Techniques*, New York/Tokyo, Weatherhill/Heibonsha, 1973. (ISBN 0-8348-0185-X)

Barrett, Timothy, *Japanese Papermaking: Traditions, Tools, Techniques*, New York/Tokyo, Weatherhill/Tankosha, 1983.

Bell, Lillian, *Plant Fibers for Papermaking*, McMinnville, Liliaceae Press, 1983. (ISBN 0-9625076-5-2)

Croft, Paul, *Stone Lithography*, London, A&C Black, 2001. (ISBN 0-7136-5056-7)

Dawson, Sophie, *The Art and Craft of Papermaking*, London, Aurum Press, 1993. (ISBN 1-85410-363-6)

Dieu Donné Hand Papermakers' Cookbook, New York, Dieu Donné Papermill, Inc., 1999.

Farnsworth, Donald, *A Guide to Japanese Papermaking*, Magnolia Editions, 1989.

Heller, Jules, *Papermaking*, New York, Watson-Guptill Publications, 1978.

Hiebert, Helen, *The Papermaker's Companion*, Pownal, Storey Books, 2000. (ISBN 1-58017-200-8)

Hunter, Dard, *Papermaking: The History and Technique of an Ancient Craft*, New York, Dover Publications, Inc., 1947. (ISBN 0-486-23619-6)

Hunter, Dard, *Papermaking in the Classroom*, Delaware, Oak Knoll Books Press, 1991. (ISBN 0-938768-24-7)

Information Dept, The Paper Federation of Great Britain, document ISBN 0-960-2496-0-5.

Kern, Marna Elyea, *The Complete Book of Handcrafted Paper*, New York, Coward, McCann & Geoghegan, Inc., 1980. (ISBN 0-698-10989-9)

Long, Paulette (ed.), *Paper – Art & Technology*, San Francisco, World Print Council, 1979. (ISBN 0-960-24960-5)

Richardson, Maureen, *Handmade Paper*, Apple Press (ISBN 0-8409-2225-7)

Robinson, Andrew, 'An Aesthetic History of Paper in Prints' in *Paper – Art & Technology*, Long, Paulette (ed.), San Francisco, World Print Council, 1979. (ISBN 0-9602496-0-5)

Sacilotto, Deli & Saff, Donald, *Printmaking: History and Process* (college paperback edn), Harcourt, Brace, Jovanovich College Publishers, 1978. (ISBN 0-03-085663-9)

Schlosser, Leonard B., 'A History of Paper' in *Paper – Art & Technology*, Long, Paulette (ed.), San Francisco, World Print Council, 1979. (ISBN 0-9602496-0-5)

Shure, Brian, *Chine Collé: A Printer's Handbook*, San Francisco, Crown Point Press, 2000. (ISBN 1-891300-15-6)

Skiold, Birgit and Turner, Sylvie, *Handmade Paper Today: A Worldwide Survey of Mills, Papers, Techniques and Uses*, London, Lund Humphries, 1989.

Takahashi, Mina (ed.), *Rags to Riches: 25 Years of Paper Art Form*, New York, Dieu Donné Papermill, Inc., 2001.

Taki, Chosuke, *Handbook on the Art of Washi*, Tokyo, Wagami-do K.K., 1991.

Tanizaki, Jun'ichiro, *In Praise of Shadows*, New Haven, Connecticut, Leete's Island Books Inc. (ISBN 0-9181-1720-2)

Turner, Sylvie, *The Book of Fine Paper*, London, Thames & Hudson, 1998. (ISBN 0-500-01871-5)

Toale, Bernard, *The Art of Papermaking*, Worcester (Mass.), Davis Publications, 1983.

Watermarks in Handmade Paper: Modern and Historic, Washington, Hand Papermaking Magazine, 2001.

Webb, Sheila, *Paper – The Continuous Thread* (Themes in Art Book), Cleveland Museum of Art and Indiana University Press. (ISBN 0-91038669-2)

Hand Papermaking is a semi-annual magazine and quarterly newsletter dedicated to advancing traditional and contemporary ideas in the art of hand papermaking. Subscriptions in the USA are $40 for one year. Call (800) 821-6604, or write to PO Box 77027, Washington, DC 20013-7027, or see www.bookarts.com/handpapermaking.

PAPER MILLS

USA

Dieu Donné Papermill, Inc.
433 Broome Street
New York, NY 11222
USA
Tel: (212) 226-0573
Fax: (212) 226-6088
Email: ddpaper@cybernex.net
www.dieudonne.org/
Dieu Donné has been a creative
centre for paper art for over 25
years. Artists can rent space and
collaborate with master papermakers on specific projects. There is
also a gallery space with ongoing
exhibitions.

Carriage House Paper
79 Guernsey Street
Brookyn, NY 11222
USA
Tel: (718) 599-PULP
Fax: (718) 599-7857
Email: chpaper@aol.com
www.carriagehousepaper.com
Carriage House Paper is a show-
room for handmade paper,
papermaking equipment and sup-
plies, and a major teaching and
papermaking facility. Donna
Koretsky is the co-founder.

Dobbin Mill
50–2 Dobbin Street
Greenpoint,

Brooklyn, New York
NY 11222
Tel: (718) 388-9631
Fax: (718) 388-9612
A papermaking studio, an artist's
book studio and a photography
darkroom. The Director of Dobbin
Mill, Robbin Ami Silverberg,
creates her own work, teaches and
works on collaborations with other
artists.

Rutgers Center for Innovative Print and Paper (RCIPP)
The Mason Gross School of the Arts
Rutgers, The State University of
New Jersey
33 Livingston Avenue
New Brunswick NJ 08901-1979
International artists are invited,
through various grants and fellow-
ships, to work at RCIPP
collaboratively on printmaking and
papermaking editions.

Pyramid Atlantic
(Helen Frederick, Director)
6001 66th Avenue
Suite 103
Riverdale
MD 20737
USA
Tel: (301) 459-7154
Email: pyrati@earthlink.net
www.pyramidatlantic.org
Founded in 1981, Pyramid Atlantic

provides access to equipment and technical expertise through rental of its paper mill and print shop. There are also workshops, master-classes, exhibitions, lectures, demonstrations, a resource library and a gallery.

JAPAN

Awagami Factory
Fuji Paper Mills
The Hall of Awa Japanese
Handmade Paper
136 Kawahigashi
Yamakawa-cho
Yoshinogawa-shi
Oe-gun, Tokushima Prefecture 779-3401
Tel: (81) 883-42-2035
Fax: (81) 883-42-6085
Email: info@awagami.or.jp
www.awagami.or.jp/

Since the late 1700s, the Fujimori family has kept alive the tradition of *Awa-washi*, Japanese paper-making. Chozo Fujimori commercialised the papermaking of *Washi*, and it was passed on to Minoru Fujimori, the seventh-generation leader of *Awa-washi*. In 1989, the Hall of Awa Japanese Handmade Paper was established as a non-profit museum, and it offers a workspace to artists from all over the world. A programme of summer workshops is organised each year. There are also handmade papers for sale.

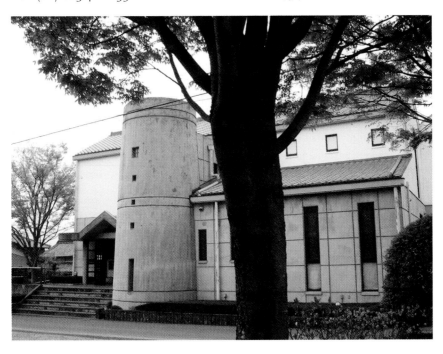

Awagami Factory, Fuji Papermill, Tokushima, Japan

UK

Scotland

The Paper Workshop
Gallowgate Studios
Top Floor
15 East Campbell Street
Glasgow G1 1DG
Scotland, UK
Tel: (44) (0)141-552-4353
Email: jacki.parry@btinternet.com
An independent papermaking studio established in 1985, the Paper Workshop welcomes invitations to lecture. Studio rental and tuition can be arranged by appointment, and collaborative projects are also considered.

Charmian Pollok
Drumlean Cottage,
Kinlochard, by Aberfoyle,
Stirling,
Scotland, UK
Tel: (44) (0)1877-387247
Fax: (44) (0)1877-387247
Email:
charmian@charmianpollok.co.uk
www.charmianpollok.co.uk
This is a rurally based papermaking workshop run by a well-established papermaker. Workshops can be arranged for all levels of groups in venues of their choice. There is papermaking at all levels, including workshops on Scottish native-plant pulps, paper arts & crafts, printmaking, book-making and pulp painting. There are also environmentally based projects for children and adults, as well as lectures and slide shows. Papermaking materials, including moulds and deckles and pulps, are available.

PULP
Paper Arts Workshop
Unit F, 41 Purdon Street,
Glasgow, G11 6AF
Scotland, UK
Email:
alison.paperprintbook@virgin.net
www.paperartsworkshop.co.uk
The workshop offers weekend courses, evening classes and a summer programme in hand-papermaking and bookbinding, with commissions, collaborative projects and pulp supply also undertaken.

England

Sophie Dawson Papermaking
Rainthorpe Hall, Tasburgh
Norwich, UK
NR15 1RQ
Tel: (44) (0)1508-470618
Fax: (44) (0)1508-470799

Maureen Richardson
Plant Papers Mill
Romilly
Brilley, nr. Hay on Wye
Tel: (44) (0)1497-831546
Herefordshire, UK
HR3 6HE
Maureen Richardson is a papermaker, author and teacher. She has produced handmade paper for sale since 1976.

PAPERMAKING SUPPLIERS

USA

Dieu Donné Papermill, Inc.
433 Broome Street
New York
NY 11222
USA
Tel: (212) 226-0573
Fax (212) 226-6088
Email: ddpaper@cybernex.net
www.dieudonne.org/
Papermaking supplies, custom
papers, workshops, gallery.

Carriage House Paper
79 Guernsey Street
Brookyn
NY 11222
USA
Tel: (718) 599-PULP
Fax: (718) 599-7857
Email: chpaper@aol.com
www.carriagehousepaper.com
Papermaking supplies, equipment,
custom paper.

Lee Scott McDonald
PO Box 264
Charlestown
MA 02129
USA
Tel: (617) 242-2505
Fax: (617) 242-8825
Papermaking supplies, equipment,
production equipment.

Twinrocker
100 East Third Street
PO Box 413
Brookston
IN 47923
USA
To order dial: 1-800-757-TWIN
(8946) or Tel: (765) 563-3119
Fax: (765) 563-TWIN (8946)
Email: twinrocker@twinrocker.com
Papermaking supplies.

Talas
568 Broadway
Suite 107
New York
NY 10012
USA
Tel: (212) 219-0770
Fax: (212) 219-0735
Email: info@talas-nyc.com
Bookbinding materials.

UK

Tony King
4 Craighouse Terrace
Edinburgh
Scotland
UK
EH10 5LJ
Tel: (44) (0)131-447-1546
Supplier of handmade moulds and
deckles.

Falkiner Fine Papers
76 Southampton Row
London
UK
WC1B 4AR
Tel: (44) (0)20-7831-1151
Fax: (44) (0)20-7430-1248
Japanese papers for chine collé.

L. Cornelissen & Son Ltd
105 Great Russell Street
London
UK
WC1B 5BH
Tel: 44 (0)20-7636-1045
Speciality art store selling artists'
pigments.

John Purcell Paper
15 Rumsey Rd
London
UK
SW9 OTR
Tel: (44) (0)20-7737-5199
Fax: (44) (0)20-7737-6765
Email: jpp@johnpurcell.net
www.johnpurcell.net
Specialist print papers.

Specialist Crafts Ltd
PO Box 247
Leicester
UK
LE1 9QS
Email: info@specialistcrafts.co.uk
www.specialistcrafts.co.uk
Tel: (44) (0)116-269-7711
Stockists of rolls of brass mesh.

Sericol Ltd
240 Seaward Street
Glasgow
G41 1NG
Scotland
UK
Tel: (44) (0)141-429-3919
Fax: (44) (0)141-429-4180
Silkscreen mesh suppliers.

INDEX